GEORGE GERSHWIN

LIVES TO

REMEMBER

Other Books by Edward Jablonski

Harold Arlen: HAPPY WITH THE BLUES

With Lawrence D. Stewart

THE GERSHWIN YEARS

George Gershwin

by Edward Jablonski

with an introduction by Harold Arlen

G. P. PUTNAM'S SONS
NEW YORK

© 1962 by Edward Jablonski

All rights reserved

Second Impression

Library of Congress Catalog Card Number: 62-10973

MANUFACTURED IN THE UNITED STATES OF AMERICA

Published simultaneously in the Dominion of Canada
by Longmans Canada Limited, Toronto

For:
(In reverse order of appearance)
Emily Rose,
Carla Leonore,
David Ira,
And their cousins,
Linda and Gary Sandy

CONTENTS

INTRODUCTION

After the hundreds of thousands of words that have been written about George Gershwin one would hesitate—and I did—when asked to write an introduction to this book. After reading Ed Jablonski's manuscript, I realized how terribly important it was to reach the many Gershwin devotees.

Having been, fortunately, a very close friend of George Gershwin at work and at play, I thought I might contribute an anecdote, but before I do perhaps I should describe George as I saw him.

His eyes and mouth were sensitive; his chin was strong; his body slender, wiry and rhythmic. In spite of the self-certainty of his own uniqueness, I always saw a questioning look—which to me meant humility. His greatness lay not only in his dynamic talent, drive and sureness, but in that questioning look.

As for the anecdote, during the mid-thirties, when so many of us—Irving Berlin, Arthur Schwartz, "Yip" Harburg, Harry Warren, the Gershwins—were in Hollywood writing for films, we used to gather at parties and would inevitably wind up at the piano. I particularly noticed George's naturalness and the feeling-at-ease quality that he had. One night, terribly anxious to find out about this, I cornered George and asked, "George, you always seem so comfortable at the piano. Don't you ever get nervous?"

There was a moment of silence, then came the blunt truth. "Of course—but I never let on."

I would like very much to point out another important truth. Every one of the great composers I've known, and this certainly holds true of George, always began—though the natural drive was there—their newest assignment as if they had never written anything before. But the challenge, ever fresh and ever new, makes music a delicious but mysterious art.

It is good to know at present, with our world so preoccupied with science that may get us nowhere, here was a young man filled with instinct and emotion who has reached out and become universal. *His* shiny inventions make the world a happier place.

HAROLD ARLEN

GEORGE GERSHWIN

Chapter 1

BIG CITY, SMALL BOY

BAREFOOT and dressed in overalls, six-year-old George Gershwin stopped short in his dash along 125th Street in New York's Harlem. Something fascinated him—an unusual, exciting sound coming from the penny arcade. Inside he found a player piano, or pianola as it was called in the early days of the century; it was clattering out popular songs and ragtime tunes in a mechanical yet hesitating manner.

Someone—not George—had dropped a nickel in the slot and George stood there, rooted in wonder, as the pianola reeled out a ragtime rendition of Rubinstein's *Melody in F* ("Welcome, sweet springtime . . ."). George watched hypnotized as the perforated paper rolled over the tracker bar and the keys pounded out a powerful, thumpy beat, decorated in the melody with tricky figurations. The old pianola stopped and started,

11

wheezed, and made a strange yet wonderful kind of music that would certainly have surprised Rubinstein.

George's attention lasted only as long as the nickel. Once it ran its course and the music stopped, George was ready to continue his restless exploration of the ever-changing, adventure-filled streets of Manhattan. In 1904 there were many horse-drawn wagons in the streets and very few automobiles. The wagons were fine for stealing rides; the ice wagons were a wonderful source of supply for dripping chunks of ice in the summertime. The bakery wagons always smelled tempting, and maybe the driver would give a small boy a cookie for watching the horse and wagon.

The streets were filled with pushcarts and men selling everything from shoes to hard, round, delicious doughnut-shaped bagels. The streets echoed with the cries of the peddlers that mingled with the sounds of George and his friends at play in the street, with the talk and laughter of the grownups, with the sound of the phonograph that stood on the sidewalk in front of the music store. These sounds blended also with the pianola's music from the arcade, with the rhythm of the crunching of wheels on the brick streets, with the clip-clop of the horses' hoofs and, from time to time, the screech and roar of the elevated train.

George didn't know it then, but he was unconsciously absorbing all these sounds and rhythms just as he did the folk songs and dances he heard at family parties and weddings.

Even though he never forgot the experience at the

penny arcade, George was not very interested in music as a boy. He was a thin, dark, nervous boy, born with an inner restlessness. His teachers complained of his inability to concentrate on his studies—and he played hooky too often to make him very popular in school. George preferred the streets—he was even roller-skating champion of Seventh Street. He played street hockey (with a stick and a tin can), he played "cat" with the neighborhood boys—and he rarely avoided a fight. Even at suppertime the sounds of a street fight would bring him running out of the house, still chewing, and ready for the fray. Often he came home, as much in triumph as defeat, with a torn shirt and a bloody nose.

His parents were worried, for it was clear that George was hardly the model boy. He even stole fruit, fat pretzels and bagels off the pushcarts. As for music, George said, "that's for maggies"—his word for sissies.

It was the word he had used one day when he had decided to play hooky again. He was twelve and a not very promising pupil in P.S. 25 in the Lower East Side. Rather than join the "maggies" who had been herded into the assembly hall to hear an eleven-year-old violinist play, George ducked out into the school-yard to play cat.

The violinist, Maxie Rosenzweig, had begun to play as George happened to run past an open window feeling free and quite superior to the captives in the assembly hall. Just as he had at the penny arcade, six years before, George stopped running and started listening.

Maxie was playing Dvořák's *Humoresque*. The music and the playing were, to George, "a flashing revelation of beauty."

Determined to meet the music maker, George waited outside the school; he couldn't go into the auditorium for fear of getting caught. It began to rain and soon George was thoroughly soaked. After waiting for an hour and a half he decided to take the chance of going into the building. Everyone, including Maxie Rosenzweig, had left. Not easily discouraged, George searched through the deserted school until he found someone in the office who gave him Maxie's address. Wet though he was, George walked to Maxie's home, rang the bell, and presented himself as a fan of the young violinist. Maxie had eluded George again, but his parents were so amused by George—of whom it might be said that everything was dampened but his spirit—that they arranged for an early meeting of the two boys.

"From the first moment," George later recalled, "we became the closest of friends. We chummed about arm in arm. . . . When we'd play hooky, we'd talk eternally about music—that is, when we weren't wrestling. I used to throw him every time, by the way, though he was one of those chubby, stocky kids."

George idolized Maxie, even though he was a year older than the boy violinist. They made impressive plans for the future: Maxie was to become a great violin virtuoso (which he did under the name of Max Rosen), and George would be his piano accompanist.

But Maxie dealt George his earliest discouraging blow. During one of their serious musical discussions he finally told George, "You haven't got it in you, Georgie. Take my word for it, I can tell." Maxie advised George to give up any plans for a musical future. Here he was already twelve and he knew absolutely nothing about music; he couldn't play any instrument. He certainly heard very little music at home, and there were no musicians in the family history. Because Pop Gershwin played Caruso records on the phonograph and occasionally entertained the family by humming into a comb wrapped with tissue paper—that didn't really count as a musical background.

The Gershwins had come from St. Petersburg (now Leningrad), Russia, in the late 1890s. Morris Gershwin was a plucky, resourceful little man with a disarming sense of humor. His arrival in America was not without a typical overtone of disaster. As his ship drew into New York harbor, Morris rushed to the rail to salute the Statue of Liberty. He succeeded only in losing his hat over the side. It was not a very impressive hat, but in the band he had placed the address of his only relative in New York.

Once landed, Morris set out to find his uncle, a tailor. He did, too, after a day's searching, in Brooklyn. Morris, however, decided to settle in the Lower East Side across the river in Manhattan. He was in almost familiar surroundings. Though New York was a great deal more metropolitan than St. Petersburg and the tempo of its living seemed much faster, Morris managed to make himself at home. He understood the language of his neighbors, most of them also recent immigrants. They shared his religious beliefs, as well as the customs, dances and songs brought with them from their homeland. America, Morris Gershwin soon learned, was not so strange and foreign a place after all.

He had been a shoemaker in Russia and found himself a job in a shoe factory. Morris was a fine and careful craftsman and was soon promoted to foreman in the factory. He was also beginning to learn the English language, a necessity once he left the Lower East Side for other parts of Manhattan.

Morris renewed his friendship, too, with pretty Rose Bruskin, a girl he had known in St. Petersburg. Rose had come to America with her family a year or two before Morris. Because he was doing so well at the shoe factory Morris felt he could afford to marry and raise a family. He convinced Rose and they were married, celebrating the event with a big, traditional, old-country wedding to which they invited all the friends and relatives they had known in Russia. It became part of family folklore in later years that the wedding had also been visited by Theodore Roosevelt, then New York's police commissioner.

It was on December 6, 1896, while the Gershwins were living over Simpson's Pawnshop, in the Lower East Side, that their first child was born; they named him Ira. When Morris changed jobs (something he was to do frequently) the Gershwins moved to Brooklyn so that he could walk to work. They lived on Snedicker Avenue directly across the street from the neighborhood synagogue. An elevated railway ran behind the house right outside the second-story window. Except for the passing trains, it was a quiet neighborhood made up mostly of middle-class Jewish families like the Gershwins.

In the little stucco house on Snedicker Avenue, George Gershwin was born on September 26, 1898. Two years later another boy was born; he was named Arthur. In 1906 a girl, Frances, joined the family.

As the first-born, Ira, it was hoped, would amount to something: a doctor, perhaps, or a teacher. Even as a young boy he read a great deal, although his parents didn't think much of his favorite reading matter, the terrible dime novels (the comic books of their time) with the garish covers. Ira also read better books when he discovered the school library.

George seemed to have no interest at all in reading —nor, in fact, little else but running in the streets with his friends. He most certainly had no interest in music until Maxie reawakened the magic George had first discovered in a Harlem penny arcade. And then Maxie had to spoil it by telling George he didn't have any music in him at all.

A piano made the difference. Not long after Maxie had given George his saddening opinion, when the Gershwins were living on Second Avenue over a phonograph shop, Rose Gershwin decided they should have a piano. It lent a touch of culture to the flat and besides, if her sister could have a piano, so could the Gershwins.

A secondhand piano was bought so that Ira, the family scholar, could take lessons. He had begun to study with his Aunt Kate, but it was soon obvious that he would shine better at words than music. "I wasn't too apt a pupil," he admitted, "and was quite content to limit my musical activity to cranking the Victrola."

As he watched the ancient upright being hoisted through the window into the Gershwin "front room," Ira felt certain he was doomed to dull piano lessons.

The moving men had barely pushed the piano up against the wall when George darted over, adjusted the stool, sat down—and actually played a popular song! The other Gershwins watched this performance, eyes popping, certain that there was some kind of magic involved. Ira Gershwin later remembered how much he was impressed with his brother's "swinging left hand" and "by harmonic and rhythmic effects" that were just as good as any he had heard played by vaudeville pianists.

"Georgie, where did you learn to play?" was the question.

"At my friend's house on Seventh Avenue," he answered. "They have a pianola. We'd put a roll on and I tried to follow it with my hands on the keys. That's how I learned the song."

Morris and Rose were astonished, for their George had never seemed to be able to stay interested in anything long enough to learn how it worked. When George actually asked to be given piano lessons, they were willing to draw the line on the miracle. They simply knew that he would never stay with that—the lessons with a teacher, the practice every day. At best, they felt, he would explore the new world of music for a couple of weeks, a month at most, and that would end Georgie's career as a pianist.

While the debate went on, Ira watched from the sidelines, interested only in learning whether or not his kid brother would be able to rescue him from a dread fate. George was persuasive and persistent. Mama Gershwin consented: Georgie would study music, not Ira.

This seemingly small family decision made on a spring day in 1910 would change the course of American musical history. And, if George Gershwin had succeeded in stunning his family that day, it was nothing compared to the effect he was to have on the world of music in just a few short years.

Chapter 2

A LITTLE SCHOOL
AND A LOT OF STUDY

G<small>EORGE</small>'s first piano teacher was a neighborhood lady, Miss Green, who charged fifty cents a lesson. In very little time George worked his way through Beyer's instruction book as well as Miss Green's knowledge of the piano and music. George had an instinctive feeling for the piano and there was no end to his curiosity and urge to know everything about music. Those very qualities that were absent from his regular schoolwork he poured into his piano study, sweeping himself along with his somewhat perplexed and not very well equipped teachers before him.

He exhausted the abilities of two more lady teachers when he met one day a pianist who "played the piano with great gusto and a barrel of gestures." Now here

was the way to play the piano, George imagined, not at
all in the sedate manner of the ladies. He was so impressed with the gusto and gestures that he asked the
flamboyant pianist the name of his teacher.

George wasted no time in presenting himself at the
gentleman's door. He turned out to be a fine-looking
man with an impressive mustache—he even looked like
a musician!—a former bandleader and conductor of
operetta. He charged the considerable sum of $1.50 a
lesson. This was a good deal of money to be spent upon
the luxury of piano lessons, but the Gershwins always
managed to have it. Pop Gershwin seemed to have a
genius for poor business ventures, which ranged from
Turkish baths to restaurants, but somehow kept the
family supplied with the necessities as well as the luxu-
ries like George's piano lessons, Ira's education and a
maid.

As for George's new teacher, "He started me on a
book of excerpts from the grand operas. In six months
I had advanced as far as the overture to *William Tell*."
His teacher's style of music making, while dramatic
and splendid to watch, actually did George's music
very little good. Luckily George, following his own
impulses, added to his musical education by attending
recitals by the great pianists of the day—Godowsky,
Bauer, Hoffman—and carefully kept his programs and
made his own musical scrapbook. He also attended
concerts in various halls all over town, literally soaking
up music. He sometimes went to hear the Beethoven
Symphony Orchestra which performed the classics in

the auditorium of P.S. 63, not far from where the Gershwins lived. One of the pianists in the orchestra, Jack Miller, was a friend of George's. He suggested that George might like to study with his teacher, a man named Charles Hambitzer.

In the spring of 1913 Jack took George with him to visit Hambitzer. It was a happy meeting for George, for he finally met a man who recognized his musical promise and who was equipped to do something about it. Their first meeting wasn't very promising, however. After Jack had introduced them, Hambitzer asked George to play for them. Delighted, George obliged. He sat down at the piano, rubbed his hands in what he thought was a very professional manner and charged into the overture to *William Tell*. His hands leaped, scampered and flashed over the keyboard, his arms waved, he all but played with his elbows, for they were in action also; George was certain he was making quite an impression.

He was.

Hambitzer, the faintest trace of a smile about his mouth, said nothing until George had finished.

"Where did you learn to play like that?" Hambitzer asked.

George told him.

"Let's hunt out that guy," Hambitzer suggested, with a twinkle in his eye, "and shoot him—and not with an apple on his head either!"

Charles Hambitzer, who had come to New York from his home in Milwaukee, where his father owned a music store, was a young man of thirty-two when he and George met. He was an excellent musician who could play several instruments, and was a fine pianist and composer. "He made me harmony-conscious," George was always to remember. Almost two years of haphazard study had done him very little musical good; and the past six months particularly did him less than good. By making him aware of harmony (the sounding of more than one musical tone at the same time), Hambitzer not only set George on the path toward becoming a good pianist, but also cultivated his musical sense—his ear—by pointing out some of the technical points of music. The sounds combined into harmony, carried along by the rhythm—the beat; for George was to learn that music exists in time. Melody, Hambitzer told George, gave the individual musical sounds meaning.

When he placed his hand upon the keyboard and pressed down two or more notes at the same time, George produced a chord in harmony. If the notes sounded together without clashing or sounding disturbing to the ear, he produced a concord; if it sounded harsh he produced a discord. Thus George learned that there were natural relationships between sounds. He was being introduced to the difficult subject of musical theory; just being able to play in a dashing manner did not make a musician.

Not only was this exploration of musical theory important to his playing, it was even more important to his composing. Though he wasn't telling anybody about it, he had begun writing songs. His first, "Since I Found You," puzzled him, for though it seemed to go along fine for a few bars it eventually seemed to get lost, didn't make musical sense, and George didn't know why. Hambitzer would teach him that.

"No watching the clock for this boy!" the teacher once reported to his sister. "He's just crazy about music and can't wait until it's time to take his lesson."

Under this proper and inspired teaching George Gershwin, onetime truant, became a real scholar. True, he had little interest in anything but music—he read very little, he'd rather see a musical than a conventional play—but he was absorbing even the most difficult musical ideas without any of the problems that attended him in public school. George was as enthusiastic about Charles Hambitzer as the teacher was about him. George even went out and "drummed up ten pupils for him." Whenever Hambitzer played in a concert George was there listening. He listened intensively, "not only with my ears, but with my nerves, my mind, my heart." And when he came home he kept the family awake as he went over at the piano the music he had heard at the concert.

He also loved popular music. "The mere sound of a rag was sufficient to set me off, flooding my imagination with different notes I heard, to produce grotesque effects." In his second song, "Ragging the Traumerei," George did this very thing with one of the piano classics of Schumann, treating it to his youthful variations in the popular ragtime style.

George also went to the theatre whenever he could afford it. For fifty cents he could sit in the second balcony at a musical comedy. It was a magical world to him.

His passion for popular music concerned Charles Hambitzer a little. "He wants to go in for this modern stuff," the teacher once said, "jazz and what not. But I'm not going to let him for a while. I'll see that he gets a firm foundation in the standard music first." This meant especially the piano music of Liszt and Chopin, with additional examples from the more modern Debussy. Hambitzer also sent George to another fine teacher of theory, Edward Kilenyi, Sr., for further studies in harmony. With Hambitzer George concentrated on the piano, for he demonstrated in every way that he would develop into a fine concert pianist.

George, besides studying music and going to school, earned extra money by working in a restaurant for four dollars a week. Morris Gershwin had become a fairly successful owner of a number of restaurants and it was hoped that George might carry on the family business. It was obvious that Ira, the bookish one, would become a teacher.

"I never liked the restaurant business," George admitted some years later. Even though he had "graduated from the kitchen to the cash register" he hardly found the sound of it as enchanting as that of the piano.

He had even graduated from grammar school and

entered the High School of Commerce. To judge from his marks, it was clear that George was not college material, so Rose and Morris Gershwin felt that at least he should be equipped for the future with some useful trade, like bookkeeping. By this time, around 1913, George was a very accomplished pianist, thanks to the instruction of Charles Hambitzer. George was selected to play the piano at Commerce for the morning exercises. And in the summer he found work as a pianist in a nearby mountain resort. Here he was asked generally to play the popular songs of the day.

As important to George's future development as the studies with Hambitzer and Kilenyi was his own discovery of the best in American popular music. There was very little of it in 1912–13 that could honestly be called good, but George found himself instinctively drawn to the work of two songwriters in particular. When he was about thirteen a new song had captivated the entire nation—and later, pretty much of the rest of the world, George included. The song was "Alexander's Ragtime Band" composed by Irving Berlin.

Another song, "You're Here and I'm Here," attracted George also. He was at his Aunt Kate's wedding when he heard the song and hurried over to the bandstand and learned that it had been written by a man named Jerome Kern.

There was something special in each song that appealed to George. He noticed that each composer wrote in his own style, which belonged to him like a trademark. George studied all the songs he could get by Berlin and Kern. Berlin's songs were rough and ready, they immediately took hold of you like a folk song. Kern's songs were fashioned with the skill of an educated musician. Berlin's melodic line—the tune—was nervous and jumpy; Kern's songs were smooth and flowing. Berlin's reflected the new style of ragtime and jazz, Kern's were almost in the classic style of the art song.

To George, who studied Berlin and Kern as keenly as he did Chopin and Debussy, this meant that for all its sometime vulgarity, American popular music was actually growing up. You could base your own style on the music of your country's people—you could borrow their crackling rhythms, their off-key harmonies and the natural flow of the language. And you could also make them good music. But George knew too that, though he might imitate the styles of Berlin and Kern in his first songs, he would not amount to anything himself until he wrote in his own way, in a Gershwin style.

In the meantime Ira was distinguishing himself in school and seemed well on his way toward a literary career. He was proving to be quite an artist, too. He and George spent little time together; the year and a half difference in their ages meant a lot to the teen-agers.

Ira was a student at Townsend Harris Hall, a pre-college school for above-average students. He was active on the school paper, for which he wrote light verse and drew sketches. He also belonged to a local literary club, the Finley Club, which met at the Christodora House in the Lower East Side. In March 1914, he talked George, whose reputation as a smart pianist was growing, into playing at one of the club's entertainments. It was George's first public appearance as both pianist and composer. He accompanied one of their young friends in a song medley and also played a piano solo, choosing as his selection his own *Tango*. He liked the attention and applause, he liked playing his own music and he felt the urge to explore the world of Irving Berlin and Jerome Kern.

At the age of fifteen, George was about to cause another crisis in the Gershwin household.

"NO!" was Mama Gershwin's answer to the request.

Her answer echoed through the flat. George had merely asked to be allowed to drop out of high school for a career in Tin Pan Alley, the center of the popular music business.

In his eager searchings he had managed to meet Mose Gumble of Jerome H. Remick & Co., a music publishing house. Mr. Gumble was so impressed with George's playing and his ability to read new music on sight that he was willing to offer him a job as a pianist on Remick's staff. There were no other fifteen-year-old pianists in Tin Pan Alley, so the offer, which included a weekly wage of $15, was very tempting. Just the thought of meeting all the famous and glamorous peo-

ple he had seen in vaudeville and musical comedies—
or better, Irving Berlin and Jerome Kern—was enough
to encourage George to play hooky forever.

But "NO!" seemed to be his mother's final answer.
Pop stayed out of it, content to watch from the sidelines. So did the rest of the family. Rose Gershwin was
firm: why should he stop his education, his preparation
for a real job, for the uncertain life of a piano player?
What future was there in music? A teacher, or an ac-
countant—now these were honest professions, but a
player of pianos in Tin Pan Alley! Whoever heard of
that?

Just as he persisted three years before and ended up
at the piano, so did George persist again. He argued
that $15 a week was a great deal of money for a boy his
age, and certainly it was much more than the $4 he
earned as the keeper of a cash register. Besides, he
didn't plan to spend his life as a "piano pounder" or a
"plugger"; he was going to compose popular songs,
good songs like those of Irving Berlin.

Mama had never heard of Berlin until George had
begun talking about him; she had, of course, heard
"Alexander's Ragtime Band." Well, George went on,
Irving Berlin was earning a very nice living in Tin Pan
Alley. So were Jerome Kern, Victor Herbert, Albert
Von Tilzer and others. Besides, he was pretty tired of
the High School of Commerce, of bookkeeping and
working in a restaurant. Music was exciting and he
knew he would do well at it.

Finally, as usual, Rose Gershwin gave in. George dropped out of the High School of Commerce in May, 1914, to start his real schooling in the tough world of American popular music.

Chapter 3

TIN PAN ALLEY

Gᴇᴏʀɢᴇ hurried along along 28th Street toward Fifth Avenue, carried along as much by his excitement as his wanting to be at work on time the first day.

Tin Pan Alley! To George it was more like the promised land. Early in the morning, however, it was quiet and it was not terribly impressive. Tin Pan Alley—West 28th Street from Broadway to Fifth Avenue—had once been a genteel residential neighborhood, lined with three- and four-story brownstone houses. It had run down; the old residents moved away and the brownstones were converted into rehearsal studios. Rents became lower as the buildings grew shabbier.

In the early 1900s the music publishers began moving in. The small rooms of the onetime fashionable brownstones were made even smaller. The publishers subdivided them into tiny cubicles (what had once been one room generally became four cubicles) on both sides of the central hallway. In each cubicle was placed a massive, usually secondhand, upright piano on which were piled all the latest songs of the publisher.

In the warm months the windows along 28th Street were open and the street reverberated with the clatter and banging of hundreds of pianos. A newspaper man, Monroe Rosenfeld, is supposed to have heard the sound of all those pianos one summer day and remarked, "It sounds like somebody pounding on tin pans." Out of this came the appropriate name Tin Pan Alley, a colorless street of shabby buildings, but to George Gershwin, its youngest piano pounder, it was a glittering, enchanting street.

George's job was to demonstrate songs to singers and dancers—anyone who could possibly use a Remick song in their vaudeville act. He literally pounded out these songs for almost ten hours a day. His skill at the piano made them sound better than they actually were. He could also "transpose" remarkably well. If a singer had difficulty reaching the high notes of a song, George transposed it to a lower key, which meant he had to play different notes from those in the printed music. Not many Alley pounders could do that.

Dancers liked what George could do with rhythm, for his playing style had a powerful drive, accuracy, and yet was also free, so that the dancer could let himself go. George took a quick liking to a very young— they were also in their mid-teens—sister-brother dancing team. The girl, Adele, was extremely pretty and bright, sang with a small voice and had a devilish sense of humor. Her brother, Fred, was an excellent, nimble dancer and also sang a little. The Astaires were just beginning in vaudeville but, like George, their goal was musical comedy. In George's cubicle at Remick's they joked and had a wonderful time. George even enjoyed Fred Astaire's piano playing. In their serious moments they talked of the future and musical comedy. George rather dreamily said one day, "Wouldn't it be great if I could write a musical show and you could be in it?"

The Astaires agreed, but returned to their vaudeville and George kept on plugging Remick songs.

During the early 1900s there was no radio, television, nor a great phonograph record industry to make a song a hit. Publishers hired pluggers to visit vaudeville houses, restaurants, hotels, the "picture houses" (where the new moving pictures were shown) and even the five-and-ten-cent stores. The plugger's beat ran from the Bowery to Broadway, and even to cities near New York with important theatres and other spots that used songs.

One of George's partners was Benny Bloom, who had gotten him the job at Remick's. During the day they demonstrated songs at the office on 28th Street; in the evenings they made the rounds of the picture houses. While the projectionist rewound the film, George and Benny took advantage of the intermission by projecting slides upon the screen on which were the words of the latest Remick song and pictures. While George played, Benny led the audience in a community sing, hoping that the customers would remember "Mary, You're a Little Bit Old-fashioned" or "Rebecca of Sunny-Brook Farm" the next time they bought sheet music or piano-rolls.

On Saturday afternoons a good spot was the Siegel-Cooper department store on Sixth Avenue at 18th Street. People loved to gather there to shop and also to hear the song demonstrations. Benny would distribute the "chorus slips," on which the words to the main part of the song—the chorus—were printed. Benny coaxed the shoppers into singing as George accompanied.

Sheet music in those days sold for ten cents a copy (six for fifty cents) and on a good day George and Benny could sell as many as a thousand copies of Remick's songs. Before they began, they took the precaution of presenting the salesgirls with bottles of perfume so that when a customer asked for the "latest song," he received one (or six, depending upon which coin he gave the girl) of Remick's latest songs.

It was a very tiresome grind for George to pound out the same old uninspired songs. After a few weeks of plugging they would go on to new songs—equally uninspired.

In his free moments George worked on his own songs, or improved his piano technique by playing Bach. This amazed his piano-pounding colleagues, most of whom played by ear and couldn't even read music.

George was neither that kind of pianist, nor that kind of composer. He was attracting a great deal of attention, in fact, as a pianist. Songwriters often dropped into Remick's just to hear him play. Among them were Irving Caesar, who hoped to become a lyric writer someday, and Harry Ruby, himself a plugger who also wanted to compose.

When George submitted some of his own songs to Jules Von Tilzer, head of Remick's professional department, he was told, "Remick's has plenty of songwriters under contract, better stick to your piano playing."

George began to feel he *was* stuck. Working in Tin Pan Alley was not what he had imagined. The songs he had to play were boring and trite; he knew he could write better tunes. He was writing them, but no one was interested.

He had been working a year at Remick's when he and a young friend, Murray Roth, collaborated on a little song with a big title, "When You Want 'Em, You Can't Get 'Em, When You've Got 'Em, You Don't Want 'Em." Remick's was still not interested in this side of George's talents, so George and Murray took it to other publishers.

They demonstrated it for Harry Von Tilzer. Sophie Tucker, the great vaudeville star, liked the song. That was enough for Von Tilzer; he decided to publish it.

The two boys tried to appear calm and businesslike as they discussed the terms. Murray asked for an advance of $15, but George decided he would like to wait for all of his royalties in a lump sum.

Murray proved to be the wiser of the two. Some months after, George went around to the Von Tilzer office and asked about his royalties. Von Tilzer reached into his pocket and handed George a five-dollar bill. It was all he ever received for his first published song.

His next one made him even happier, for the sheet music bore the title of a real Broadway show, *The Passing Show of 1916*. Though George was not particularly proud of the song, a little fast number he had practically tossed off, the fact that it was a show song, a production number, was enough for him.

"It was now," he later recalled, "that the popular-song racket began to get definitely on my nerves. Its tunes somehow began to offend me. Or perhaps my ears were becoming attuned to better harmonies. At any rate I was a most unhappy lad at Remick's. I decided to leave after having been with them for over two years."

He walked into the office of his superior, Mose Gumble, and announced that he was through. Mr. Gumble wasn't very much surprised, for it was obvious to him that a boy with George's talents would never remain a Tin Pan Alley piano pounder for very long. He wished George well and asked him just one question, "Where are you going from here?"

"I don't know," was George's honest answer.

"Once out of Remick's I scarcely knew which way to turn." After a few weeks of doing nothing, he heard

that the City Theatre on 14th Street needed a pianist.
George hurried over and was hired to play for the
supper show—that is, while the musicians in the orchestra had their supper, George filled in for them to accompany the acts.

Happy to be working, he conscientiously attended
the morning's rehearsals and even the matinee to get a
good idea of how the show went. He was anxious, as
usual, to be very good at his work.

"The supper show began," he was to relate some
years after with a shudder. "I got along fine with three
or four acts. I was especially good with a turn that used
Remick's songs. Then came what I consider the most
humiliating moment of my life."

An act came on that required special music. In it
were a leading lady, a leading man, a comedian and
six chorus girls. George had to play their music from
pages of loose and messy manuscript paper. Not only
did he have to play, he also had to keep an ear and an
eye out for special cues. Somewhere in the act he
missed a cue. He found himself playing one thing as
the chorus girls sang another.

Realizing what had happened, George could feel
panic setting in. His face turned crimson especially
"when it came to my mind that the City Theatre was
in my neighborhood and that there might be some people out in the audience who knew me—not to mention
proud members of my family and a few relations."

Worse was yet to come. About this time the comedian saw an opportunity to take advantage of the situ-

ation. He shouted across the footlights at the hapless George, "Who told you you were a piano player? You ought to be banging the drums!"

George stopped playing. "The act went on," he recalled later, "without any music—with the chorus girls giggling, the comedian still joking and the audience howling with laughter."

After the show was over, George slunk out of the theatre, hoping no one noticed him, the horrible, mocking, laughter still burning his ears. He stopped at the box office and told the cashier, "I was the piano player this afternoon and I'm quitting." He left without collecting his day's wages.

He found other work, he played at parties with a banjoist, he played in a small band in a Brooklyn cabaret, and best of all, that winter he was hired as a rehearsal pianist for a new show, *Miss 1917*, which was being prepared for production.

As rehearsal pianist George would accompany the dancers and singers for hours on end, much as he had done at Remick's. But there was a great difference. *Miss 1917* was a Broadway show with the songs composed by Jerome Kern and Victor Herbert. To nineteen-year-old George it was a wonderful experience, meeting his hero, playing the songs in the show and learning how a show was put together.

Miss 1917 was not fated to run very long at the Century Theatre, though George made the switch from rehearsal pianist to accompanist for the Sunday night concerts that were held at the same theatre. One night when George accompanied Vivienne Segal, star of *Miss 1917,* she introduced two of his songs. He and Irving Caesar had collaborated on "You-oo, Just You" and "There's More to the Kiss Than the X-X-X," in which the singer imitated the sound of a kiss. It was a clever idea and Miss Segal had liked it; so did Remick's who decided to publish the song.

George, however, found he could not exist on his royalties and he did not want to depend upon his parents for his spending money. He did live at home, but he felt he should not be a burden. He was in demand as a rehearsal pianist, and for a short time he even worked as a pianist in a theatre pit band, but the show didn't last. He was also regarded as a fine accompanist and worked a lot as pianist for vaudeville singers.

Louise Dresser, one of the most popular singers at the time, hired him to make a vaudeville tour with her. It was George's first taste of the Big Time. They opened in New York, went on to Boston, to Baltimore and finally to Washington, D. C.

It was the first week of March 1918—Preparedness Week in the capital geared for war. Miss Dresser and George were thrilled to learn one night that President Wilson, a vaudeville fan, was in their audience. They returned the gesture by patriotically marching in the Preparedness Parade.

Miss Dresser was very pleased with Georgie, as she called him, for not only was he a superb accompanist, but he strove continually to be better. He had a piano put in his hotel room and practiced all the time. This drive for perfection, evident early in George, was an important factor in his life.

While all this was most exciting and gave him valuable experience, it was not what George really wanted. He kept himself in song writing trim by composing all the time, but had managed to get only three of his songs published and a few sung in public. He composed tunes that were set to lyrics by Irving Caesar, by a good friend, Lou Paley, and, more importantly, by his big brother Ira. None of these three were yet professional lyricists. Caesar worked in an automobile factory, Paley was a teacher.

As for Ira, he had suffered an unfortunate collision with chemistry at City College. This naturally closed his medical career—then "when I heard that calculus was in the offing, I decided to call it an education."

He began to work at all sorts of jobs, from desk clerk in his father's Turkish baths to shipping clerk in a department store. Stimulated by George's industry, and because he had a natural flair for words, Ira decided that he too would try his hand at song writing.

If George liked Ira's lyric, he would set it to music. Or if he did a tune for which Ira came up with a good title and lyric idea they would collaborate on a song.

One that George liked was "The Real American Folk Song (Is a Rag)," which Ira had devised during the quiet hours while tending the St. Nicholas Baths for his father.

Nora Bayes, a top vaudeville personality, had liked one of George's songs, "Some Wonderful Sort of Someone," and wanted it for her new show, *Ladies First*. George also offered her "The Real American Folk Song," which she also liked. It was the first George and Ira Gershwin song ever heard in a musical.

Not only did she like George's songs, Miss Bayes also liked his playing. So when *Ladies First* went on its try-out tour, the out-of-town performances before playing New York, George went along as her accompanist. The temperamental Miss Bayes, however, began to object to George's playing, which was quite tricky at times. Not only did it tend to throw her off now and then, it stole some of the spotlight from her. Worse, George even refused to change the ending of one of his songs for her.

The team of Bayes and Gershwin could not last. She was a vaudeville headliner and he was just a kid pianist who wrote songs. George left and returned to New York.

This time his move was not so drastic, however. He actually had another job. Many months before he went on the brief, ill-fated tour with Nora Bayes he had been signed to a contract by the publishing firm T. B. Harms Company.

Max Dreyfus of Harms had been told of George Gershwin, a fine pianist and an interesting and promising composer. He arranged to see George one day and listened to his songs. Though he didn't agree to publish any of them, Mr. Dreyfus did place George on the staff of Harms as a composer. For $35 a week he had nothing to do but drop by the office now and then with a song.

It took Harms over half a year to publish even one of the dozens of songs George supplied them. The song was "Some Wonderful Sort of Someone," which introduced him to the fiery Nora Bayes.

He stalked into the Harms office after he had returned to New York. He was not in a happy mood. He was twenty and had already spent five years in Tin Pan Alley. All he had gotten out of it was a lot of hard work, a series of hard knocks and only five published songs. One a year! His creative career was not advancing very fast. Where was that show that he, Adele and Fred Astaire had dreamed about?

An unsmiling George confronted Max Dreyfus on an autumn day in 1918. Mr. Dreyfus seemed not to notice but he did have some news for George.

"George," he told him, "I have a job for you. Would you like to write songs for a musical comedy?"

Chapter 4

MUSICAL COMEDY—HITS
AND FLOPS

Finally, George could feel his professional life was taking a good turn. He was not even discouraged when he learned that the musical Mr. Dreyfus had lined up for him was not a "book show" (a musical with a plot), but a revue. Nor was he expected to do much work, for only five or so songs were required. What was really important to George was that when the posters were printed up they read: MUSIC BY GEORGE GERSHWIN.

It had come about rather simply. Max Dreyfus had a reputation for lending a hand to young producers as well as beginning songwriters. A Mr. Perkins had outlined his idea for a revue in which he planned to star his friend, the comedian Joe Cook, who, in turn, would bring in a troupe of comedians. Mr. Perkins had brought some scenic effects from Paris, even a few songs. All he needed were a handful of new songs and, of course, money.

Max Dreyfus supplied him with both.

George composed a half dozen songs for which Perkins devised some lyrics; even Ira lent a hand in one of the songs. For George the work went quickly. He was a rapid worker and always managed to keep several songs ahead of the lyric writers. He was, naturally, impatient to see *Half Past Eight* in real production, to have its out-of-town tryout and then open in New York with the posters all over Broadway declaring:

MUSIC BY GEORGE GERSHWIN

The score was completed, a routine devised, the cast was assembled. It had everything—even a bicycle act—except the "Broadway Chorus!" as the posters proclaimed. The brave little band left for Syracuse, N. Y., for its tryout. Perkins was jubilant, for he learned that opening night, December 9, 1918, had been bought out completely by a club. To George it seemed to be a happy omen at the very beginning of his career as a composer of show music.

The glittering, long-hoped-for opening night finally came, but it barely glimmered. Even the easily pleased club members who had bought out the first night were not fooled. When the curtain came down on the first half of the show they hissed. It was obvious that they were not seeing much of a show that night. Not only had the curtain not gone up at half past eight (it was closer to nine), but it went down soon after it finally did go up. It was plain that they were not getting their money's worth. Besides, where was that famous "Broadway Chorus!"?

Sensing that the show was in trouble, George came up with a last-minute suggestion. Perhaps they could keep the audience through the finale—which, he knew, came much too soon after the second-act curtain went up.

Since there were a number of comedians in Joe Cook's troupe, why not draft them to be the Broadway chorus? Perkins was doubtful, but he listened. Dress the comedians, George went on, in Chinese pajamas and send them on stage holding large umbrellas. They could improvise a routine, and perhaps the audience would not be the wiser: here would be their chorus. The desperate Perkins was willing to try anything.

George was not aware that the umbrellas Perkins had bought were of cheaply made paper. At the finale the disguised comedians moved as gracefully as they could onto the stage, but the audience wasn't fooled. Three of the umbrellas simply didn't open. The curtain came down to more hissing and catcalls.

Variety, the trade paper of show business, was devastating. Its review of *Half Past Eight* was headlined:

$2 SHOW NOT WORTH WAR TAX

By the Wednesday matinee it was clear that *Half Past Eight* was more than half gone. Each performance attracted fewer people. Even the performers were becoming reluctant; one, certain there would be no salary at the end of the week, refused to go on. Perkins could not talk him into staying and was quite desperate again, when George walked into the theatre. It was the middle of the day and he wore a blue suit and hadn't bothered to shave. Perkins rushed over.

"George, you've got to go on!" he pleaded.

"What, why?" was all that George could stammer.

"One of the acts just refused to appear and we must have something to go on while we make a change of scene."

That made sense, but George could only ask, "What will I do?"

"Play some of your hits," suggested Perkins.

What hits?

George went onstage, still in his blue suit and needing a shave, sat down at the piano. The audience was at least curious; *this* looked like a different act. On the spot George hastily made up a medley of some of the songs he had written. Finished, he walked off. The mystified audience didn't even applaud.

George managed to get his return fare to New York from Perkins and left the next day. *Half Past Eight* creaked out a few more miserable performances—five in all—before it collapsed.

Back in New York, George turned to his harmony studies and continued trying to get his songs into shows. He managed to get one, "I Was So Young," into a show titled *Good Morning, Judge.* The show opened in the spring of 1919. It became quite popular and attracted attention to George.

Among those who had liked "I Was So Young," as well as some of George's other songs, was Alex Aarons, who ran a clothing store but was more interested in the musical theatre. His father was an important man in show business and Alex hoped to follow him. Unlike most who hoped to be a Broadway producer, Alex Aarons actually knew something about music. He could appreciate what George was trying to do in the realm of popular song.

Alex decided to quit the clothing business to produce a musical show, and he would ask this George Gershwin he knew so little about to write the songs. Alex's father did not approve; it was a mistake, he argued, to commission a score from an unknown and inexperienced composer. Why get Gershwin when you could get Victor Herbert?

His mind made up, Alex chose to ignore his father's no doubt wise advice. He asked George to compose songs for the musical comedy *La La Lucille,* a book show. It was a silly little show, but it was amusing. Into it George not only poured some delightful new songs, but he also salvaged a couple that had been given no chance in *Half Past Eight,* and one that he had written five years before while he was still working at Remick's. It was one of the best songs in the show and one of George's best songs: "Nobody But You."

No out-of-town death for *La La Lucille*. It opened in New York on May 26, 1919, and enjoyed a run of over a hundred performances. Some critics even noticed that the music was fresh and original. George took pride in this and could feel at last that he was on the right path.

The following year he composed the music for the first of what was to become a series of five *George White's Scandals*. George White was a young dancer who decided to challenge the great Florenz Ziegfeld as the producer of lavish revues. In 1919 White produced the first *Scandals,* based on the Ziegfeld type of revue. The emphasis was upon the comedian and the dancing star. The chorus was made up of the loveliest girls that could be found, all decked out in the costliest, most beautiful costumes that could be found. Although George White did not have the Ziegfeld touch, he did produce a show that proved popular.

It is doubtful, however, that he would have signed George as his composer on the strength of a few published songs and the modest success of *La La Lucille*. In show business, nothing is so truly convincing as a big success, and when George applied for the job as composer of the *Scandals,* he had a big success ringing in his ears. It rang, in fact, in just about everyone's ears, George White's included, for George had tossed off one of the biggest song hits of 1920.

It started with a lunch he and Irving Caesar had, and continued on the Riverside bus ride as they went up to

the Gershwin apartment in upper Manhattan. Irving
was determined to write a "hit song," and George,
after his recent sad experiences, was not one to dis-
agree.

In the Gershwin apartment they found that there
was a card game going on in the living room. But that
disturbed them only a little as they worked at the piano
in an alcove. In fact, their playing and singing disturbed the card players (especially, for some reason, the
losers) who shouted for silence.

Despite the hubbub, George and Irving completed
the song that evening. They then performed it for the
card players, George at the piano, Irving singing and
Pop Gershwin on the musical comb. It was a catchy
song and everyone joined in,

> *Swanee,*
> *How I love you,*
> *How I love you,*
> *My dear old Swanee.*

Al Jolson heard George play and sing it at a party
and was so excited by its drive that he knew he had to
have "Swanee" as his special number. He interpolated
it into his show then running at the Winter Garden
Theatre on Broadway; he recorded it—and George and
Irving Caesar were on their way. Sheet music sales
reached a million copies in just a couple of months and
Jolson's record sold twice that number. When George
went to see George White about composing songs for

the next *Scandals,* White signed him immediately. He had heard of George Gershwin. With the sheet music of "Swanee" on the piano in practically every parlor in the country, who hadn't?

Chapter 5

WHAT IS THIS THING CALLED "JAZZ"?

Wɪᴛʜ the Twenties the Jazz Age had begun. The Twenties had not yet begun to roar, but it was beginning to be heard. The strange new sound that everyone was dancing to was called "jazz."

In later years historians would write that during the Jazz Age, the 1920s, America went on one long, noisy, ten-year joyride. The energies that had not been poured into the World War had to go somewhere. So did all the money that had piled up during the war; it was waiting to be spent on the many things you could not get in wartime; you could invest it, too, in stocks and in businesses. One of the businesses into which both money and energy were poured was entertainment.

It seemed to some worried observers that all Americans wanted to do was to have fun and make money. The world's problems did not interest them; they had had enough of that with the war. They were much more interested in dancing and taking up where they had left off when the war began. The Turkey Trot and the Cakewalk made way for the wicked Shimmy, and later the Charleston. The music for these dances was called, often as not incorrectly, "jazz."

During the Twenties practically all music that was nervous, raucous, fast—"peppy," they called it—was called jazz.

Actually, jazz was a form of folk music brought by Negro bands up the Mississippi River from New Orleans to St. Louis, Chicago, and other cities to the north. Eventually the music and the bands arrived in New York, just before the Twenties began. Jazz was an exciting music; it was often made up on the spur of the moment (improvised) by musicians who did not read music well, or at all. It was music of great vitality and rhythmic drive; it used instruments in ways they had never been used before; it often produced music of great beauty, especially in the melancholy, haunting "blues." Jazz musicians played in a free and easy manner, shifting the beat to the unexpected notes ("syncopation") and playing tones as they felt them and which could not actually be written down. It was an inventive, new and honest kind of music making.

To George it was a true expression of the American people. It was rhythmically free, its harmonies were unusual; he could not agree that it was an evil music that would lead the nation to doom. Nor was jazz purely Negro; it borrowed from the music of the white man. Spirituals, for example, out of which the blues had grown, were actually a Negro adaptation of southern hymn tunes. To George, it seemed to be a wonderful mixture of many kinds of music. What made it more wonderful was the endless flow of ideas from such jazz musicians as King Oliver, Louis Armstrong, Jelly Roll Morton, blues singer Bessie Smith and others.

The blues especially attracted George. These "sorrow songs," which were often improvised as the vocalist sang, expressed personal sadness in a mocking, humorous manner. The melodies were unforgettable. As early as 1914, just about the time he had begun work as a piano pounder at Remick's, George found himself drawn toward one of the first published blues, "St. Louis Blues," composed by a great Negro composer, W. C. Handy.

George carefully studied the blues and other jazz forms. He absorbed their musical devices—the offbeat rhythms, their powerful drive, the "blue notes"—and, more importantly, absorbed the very feeling of jazz. He felt that here was a genuine American music that could be of great inspiration to anyone who wanted to be a genuine American composer.

George had made up his mind to become just that. Many had claimed that there was no such thing as a true American music, that practically all American music was borrowed from Europe, even our so-called folk music. Now here was jazz—and there was no mistaking it when you heard it. It was American music.

George did not try to "write" jazz; no one could actually do that. The jazz musicians played it, they never wrote it. Only the phonograph record could capture a jazz performance with any accuracy. George, however, wrote music with a jazz feeling. To this he added all he had learned in Tin Pan Alley, as well as in his formal music study. In addition he added himself to his work, his gift, his drive for wanting to write music more than anything else.

In 1920, possibly earlier, George began to experiment with compositions that were certainly not songs. As part of his harmony course with Edward Kilenyi he wrote a movement or two for string quartet. He turned out a number of short piano pieces he called "novelettes." His talent was not to be confined to the thirty-two bars of a popular song.

His first chance to try out this talent came from an unexpected quarter. When he and the lyricist B. G. "Buddy" DeSylva were working on the songs for the 1922 edition of the *Scandals,* they had an idea for a one-act opera, a jazz opera, in fact, inspired by the by now country-wide popularity of jazz and jazz bands.

At first producer George White was against the idea, since he felt it would add more costs to the production for a set and costumes; besides there was the problem of a white cast getting into blackface and out again in time for the next act.

About three weeks before the *Scandals* was due to

open, White changed his mind. Maybe it wasn't such a bad idea—it would add a touch of daring culture to the *Scandals*.

For five days and nights George and Buddy worked on their little opera, *Blue Monday*. George was practically ill of overwork and anxiety. He always dated his later illnesses, his nervousness which he called "composer's stomach," from *Blue Monday*. He was especially concerned about the critical reaction to what was actually his first try at a "serious" work. How would it be received? He wasn't too certain how it would go in such a light entertainment as the *Scandals* supplied.

There was nothing particularly fancy about *Blue Monday;* its quite obvious, though tragic, plot was set in Harlem's 135th Street. For it George composed almost a half hour's continuous music, complete with arialike songs, recitative and musical interludes as in conventional opera. *Blue Monday* broke with operatic traditions in that George used touches of popular music and jazz and the story was built around Negroes. Here was probably the first, if crude, attempt at writing a native America opera. And although the parts were played by whites in blackface, and while there were the usual racial stereotypes, the Negro was treated nonetheless as a human being and not a comic figure.

George's "composer's stomach" had told him true; *Blue Monday* lasted for one whole performance once the *Scandals* opened in New York. The audience was puzzled and most of the critics were downright hostile. What was the dismal thing doing in the middle of a silly entertaining little revue? George White cut it out before the second night.

George Gershwin, however, liked to recall what one critic had predicted: "This opera will be imitated in a hundred years." It also made an impression on the bandleader for that year's *Scandals;* he never forgot it either. He was well on his way also and believed that in George Gershwin America had a composer of great genius. The bandleader was Paul Whiteman.

Jazz was in the air, indeed. No one could escape it, not even serious musicians, many of whom were fascinated by it but who learned that they simply could not play it. Jazz bands were soon heard in almost every cabaret and hotel.

Jazz was soon important enough in American life to be denounced in newspaper editorials and from the pulpit. Before long the nation was all but divided into two warring camps, one for and the other against jazz. It made little difference that neither actually knew what jazz was. To most, jazz was merely popular music, or dance music.

It was this fussing that inspired Eva Gauthier, a fine concert artist, to set the serious musical world on its ear. With all the talk about jazz and the sudden widespread attention being given to American popular song, she decided that at her next recital in Aeolian Hall she would sing popular songs along with the classic songs.

She called it a "Recital of Ancient and Modern Music for Voice," and held this history-making event on

November 1, 1923. The first part of her concert was made up of typical serious songs. In this portion she was accompanied by her pianist, Max Jaffe, who played with the proper air of decorum and dignity.

When she came to her "American" song group, Miss Gauthier opened with Irving Berlin's "Alexander's Ragtime Band," shouting out in a manner that shocked the usual Aeolian Hall audience. She followed that with Jerome Kern's "The Siren's Song," then Walter Donaldson's "Carolina in the Morning" and finally a group of three songs—"I'll Build a Stairway to Paradise," "Innocent Ingenue Baby" and "Swanee"—composed by her special accompanist for that part of the program, a slim, inventive young pianist by the name of George Gershwin.

When she was planning her recital, Eva Gauthier had gone to her friend, a onetime music critic turned novelist, Carl Van Vechten. If anyone knew what was going on in the world of the arts it was Carl Van Vechten. Miss Gauthier explained the idea she had for the recital, an idea that Van Vechten immediately approved of. But Miss Gauthier was certain that she would require a special pianist for her "American" song group, someone at home with popular music, jazz and the classics. Van Vechten had only one suggestion, "Get George Gershwin!"

During the Jazz Age parties were important to the arts, and no one gave more exciting parties than the Carl Van Vechtens. All the celebrated writers, artists, poets, composers, songwriters and musicians (serious and jazz) were there. George was a frequent guest and it took very little coaxing to get him to the piano. Once there he could play for hours. He generally played his own songs, but with such imagination and verve that no one ever tired of it. It was clear right away to Carl Van Vechten that the pianist Eva Gauthier sought was George.

At the recital he was a sensation. He was a little nervous at first in his black tie, though he did present a handsome picture. Miss Gauthier was striking in a dress that she wore backward, for dramatic effect. It was a time when formal wear for women had low necks and high backs; Eva Gauthier merely switched it. With a spotlight on her face it seemed that all that was onstage was her disembodied head and a handsome young pianist. It was very jazzy, indeed.

George spiced up the songs with rhythms that seemed to get tangled with one another and then went their separate ways. He wove in little jazzlike tricks that crackled and sparkled with humor. He played with great sureness and poise, as if he had been playing on the recital stage for years instead of the first time.

The distinguished, sophisticated audience was delighted. Instead of objecting to the singing of Tin Pan Alley songs in dignified Aeolian Hall they cheered and demanded more.

As an encore Miss Gauthier obliged with George's most recent hit—he actually could come out now and play some of his hits! The song was the properly titled "Do It Again." George and Miss Gauthier did do it again, in Boston, where they received the same enthusiastic reception.

At a single stroke George was introduced to the concert stage as both pianist and composer. He proved that he and his songs, and other good popular songs as well, belonged there as representatives of American music.

"I consider this," Carl Van Vechten declared, "one of the very most important events in American musical history. . . . Mind you, I prophesy that the Philharmonic will be doing it in two years."

Within a year George's work had inspired two prophecies: the first, that his Negro opera would be imitated in a hundred years and the second, that his kind of music would be played by no less than the Philharmonic orchestra within two years.

The prophets were wrong only in one respect: at the rate that George was going, it would not take all that time. To George even two years was a long time. George Gershwin, American composer, was in a hurry.

Chapter 6

THE "BIRTH" OF
AMERICAN MUSIC

A DANCE band in a concert hall devoted to "serious" music did not make musical sense, but it certainly helped to bring in a good crowd. Eva Gauthier, with George's assistance, had shown that it could be done. Now Paul Whiteman, "The King of Jazz," had chosen Lincoln's Birthday, 1924, to present a full concert of jazz featuring his word-famous jazz band. He did not call it a jazz concert; instead he titled his concert "An Experiment in Modern Music." Whiteman was actually not as interested in trying to play jazz as he was in demonstrating modern musical trends with the emphasis upon American music.

Aeolian Hall, where the experiment was to be held, was as staid and, yes, as stuffy in 1924 as the Metropoli-

tan Opera House is believed to be today. Since the Gauthier recital and the Whiteman concert, however, such
events have become commonplace. But in 1924 it was
shocking.

Aeolian Hall was hot that February 12th afternoon;
it was stuffed with curiosity seekers, musicians, songwriters, famous composers, friends and relatives of all
concerned, and Paul Whiteman fans—which included
some of the most serious musicians in the world.

The concert began to pall as the afternoon dragged
on. What started out to be fun—listening to the
Whiteman band reproduce examples of their idea of
primitive jazz and comparing it with their more sophisticated brand—after a while took on a quality of same-
ness. Besides, Paul Whiteman was giving his glittering
Aeolian Hall audience practically the same program he
gave them nightly at the Palais Royale, a cabaret—this
was before the era of night clubs—where New Yorkers
flocked to Charleston.

But in Aeolian Hall they had to remain seated and
just listen. The program was too long; it seemed to be
a musical lecture and not the entertaining afternoon
all had expected.

Some of the less hardy sensation seekers began to slip
out of the exits into the snowy early evening. The program had begun at three o'clock and here it was five
and not much had really happened. Perhaps Paul
Whiteman was a madman—as many of his friends had
hinted—to try a full concert of jazz in Aeolian Hall.
He did better in the dance hall.

Portly, rotund Paul Whiteman sensed that the excitement was wearing off; he wondered, too, if his friends had been right and he wrong. He had already lost several thousand dollars on the concert even though the hall was filled to capacity. He had given many tickets away and had lavished money on printing an elaborate program and other fine touches. Oh well, only two numbers to go and the "Experiment" would be over, and to judge from the less than enthusiastic applause, he could go back to dance music and leave the education to others.

Although it was a great publicity stunt, the Whiteman Aeolian Hall concert did have its educational value. He felt that what had long passed for American music was nothing more than a reflection of European music, composed by men generally educated in Europe, with European tastes and prejudices. If American music was to mean anything, Whiteman reasoned, it must reflect American ideas, American tempos, and it must be written by Americans who understood what American music actually was. Whiteman hoped that his concert would define American music.

In Europe it was a common practice for a serious composer to draw upon his country's folk music for ideas, for tunes and rhythms, and to adapt them to his own use. If he was a great enough composer, he actually succeeded in composing music that truly mirrored his country in music. Music didn't have to say it in so many words, but somehow it did say something honest and emotionally expressive of its people. In England, the gruff and wonderful Ralph Vaughan Williams carefully studied the songs of English farmers and literally made symphonies of them. In Hungary, the burning, intense little man, Béla Bartók, was using peasant music he found in out-of-the-way villages to create some of the most powerful and original music of the twentieth century.

Why not jazz, Whiteman thought, the most American of all music, as the inspiration for a new American music?

Whiteman's jazz was not improvised, of course; it was a dance-band arrangement, written out and played almost exactly the same way every time. This was, in fact, something it held in common with the music of the European concert hall. From traditional jazz Paul Whiteman and his arrangers, particularly a brilliant one named Ferde Grofé, borrowed certain elements: those decorations that in later years came to be called "hot licks," syncopation and blues harmonies. The "blue note" gave the music a kind of bittersweet quality. This was a very typical American sound found not only in the blues of the Negro, but also in the folk songs of the Appalachian Mountains and even in cowboy songs.

Instruments were used in unusual ways. There was the muted trumpet which, when an object such as a bowler hat was placed over its bell, could make an appealing *waa-waa* sound; there was the saxophone which jazzmen could make moan, bleat and sob. Instruments were used to imitate animal sounds (in a

number titled "Livery Stable Blues") and behaved
unlike the instruments in a respectable band. The emphasis on rhythm brought new celebrity to the percussion section, the drums, the banjo, and even the
once-romantic piano was employed as a rhythm instrument.

These were the most obvious devices borrowed from
jazz, those easiest to reproduce. Whether or not it was
actually true jazz that Paul Whiteman played is no
longer of any importance. The concert did make an
important contribution to the definition of American
music. It even brought serious attention to American
music, as a reflection of a country and its people, and
it focused serious attention on that forgotten man, the
American composer. It proved too that a valid American music could be based upon folk music.

Paul Whiteman's problem was to find the American
composer who could carry all this off. Remembering
back a couple of years to the *Scandals* of 1922 and *Blue
Monday,* Whiteman was sure he had found that composer in George Gershwin.

George was coming up next in the program—it was
now all up to him.

Chapter 7

THE RHAPSODY IN BLUE

IN THE wings George was as restless as the audience out front. He had learned a lot about showmanship in the musical comedy theatre and it seemed to him not a very good idea to give an audience too much, even of a good thing.

He wished, rather wistfully, that he had had more time to work on what was to be his contribution to the "Experiment." Here it was, the afternoon of the concert, the hall was filled with some of the most important personalities of the music world and the piece he was about to play was not even completely written out.

It had started a little over a month ago. Ira had been reading the New York *Tribune.* His eye was attracted to a brief item on the amusement page. WHITEMAN JUDGES NAMED, it read. COMMITTEE WILL DECIDE "WHAT IS AMERICAN MUSIC."

Lot of talk about American music these days, Ira mused, so he read on:

Among the members of the committee of judges who will pass on "What Is American Music" at the Paul Whiteman concert to be given at Aeolian Hall, Tuesday afternoon, February 12, will be Serge Rachmaninoff, Jascha Heifetz, Efrem Zimbalist and Alma Gluck.

Very high-powered names, he thought. Ira continued reading:

Leonard Leibling, editor of *The Musical Courier*, will be chairman of the critics' committee, which is to be composed of leading musical critics of the United States.

This question of "just what is American music?" has aroused a tremendous interest in music circles and Mr. Whiteman is receiving every phase of manuscript, from blues to symphonies.

Then one name leaped off the page: George Gershwin. The item concluded:

George Gershwin is at work on a jazz concerto, Irving Berlin is writing a syncopated tone poem and Victor Herbert is working on an American suite.

Ira knew that George was working on a new show score. It was not like him to keep anything secret. There were some of their friends who jokingly complained that they were so familiar with the songs for a new show that by the time the show opened they thought they were seeing a revival. George had certainly not been playing a jazz concerto around the Gershwin house.

"Are you working on a jazz concerto?" Ira asked George.

"A what?"

"A jazz concerto. It says here"—waving the paper at George—"you're writing one for the Paul Whiteman concert at Aeolian Hall."

The mystery deepened. George didn't have any idea that Paul was planning a concert. He phoned Whiteman.

"Yes, it's true, George," Paul informed him. "I've been talking about giving a jazz concert for a long time. Too long, I guess; Vincent Lopez heard about it and now he's planning one, too. I had to push my date ahead to beat him to the punch. Whoever's first will make the big splash."

"But Paul," George broke in, "the paper says I'm composing a concerto or something for the concert. Today is January 4th—the concert is just a few weeks away! How could I possibly do it? Besides, I'm tied up with Buddy DeSylva on our show. We open in Boston in a few days. I'd never have the time to toss something off for your concert, even if I wanted to."

"George," Whiteman countered, "you composed a one-act opera in five days—and I thought it was wonderful. You can do it again. I know you can."

"Maybe we did do *Blue Monday* in a hurry—we had

to—but I've never been the same ever since. Why, my composer's stomach . . ."

"Composer's stomach?"

"Sure," George went on, always ready to discuss the state of his health with anyone. "I get all tied up in knots, nervous, I have to eat only certain foods and—well, never mind that, I still don't think I could write anything for your concert. There just isn't any time."

This didn't sound final enough for the persistent Whiteman. He continued talking as if he hadn't heard George. "How long have you thought—even dreamed —about writing a piece longer than a thirty-two-bar song? Now here's your chance. Just think, a fancy audience in Aeolian Hall. It's bound to make news!"

"Paul, there just isn't any time to compose the thing. I don't really have anything in the works now except songs. I certainly don't have any idea for the kind of piece for your concert. And, if I did, there wouldn't be time to orchestrate it—and I really don't know too much about that."

"Don't worry," Whiteman assured him, sensing a reluctance on George's part to release the idea in spite of all the obstacles there were and George's arguments against it.

"We could get Ferde to orchestrate," Whiteman continued. "Just write out a piano copy and Ferde will do an orchestration that will suit the boys in the band. Some of them can do some pretty remarkable things."

"I don't know, Paul."

"Give it a try, George. We might have a lot of fun."

"I'll see if I can come up with something, Paul. But I have my doubts. Yet—maybe something could be worked up."

"I know it can, and you're the one who can do it!"

"Maybe," George was already thinking aloud over the phone. "Maybe I could try a jazz piece, or a blues . . . No concerto, though, Paul."

"Great! Whatever you want."

George was beginning to warm up to the crazy venture himself. Whiteman's enthusiasm and faith in him were contagious.

"I've got to go to Boston tomorrow, Paul. When I get back I'll call you and let you know what I've decided."

"Fine, George. Call me as soon as you get back."

On the train to Boston George thought about a concert work—and having it played in Aeolian Hall! It was an exciting idea, and certainly he had long dreamed of such a thing. The rhythm of the train's wheels stimulated him. He once said, "I hear music in the heart of noise."

Maybe growing up in New York, with its traffic, its rush, its glitter, had something to do with that. The distractions that forced others to look for peace and quiet hardly bothered him at all. The nervous tempo of a great and magic city—his America—excited him; its music was different from any that had ever been heard.

The train roared into Boston as George imagined the kind of a composition he might do for Paul Whiteman. Why not an "American Rhapsody"? Not a bad title, he felt. And if it were a rhapsody, he would not have to be worried too much about its strict musical form. He could allow the music to go its own way, as his own imagination dictated and not as it was decreed in the books on music.

When he returned from Boston he had outlined the complete work in his mind. He would open it with a rousing whoop—that would be a real "icebreaker." (An icebreaker in the world of musical comedy was the exciting opening number of a show that immediately captured the attention of the audience.) In his opening, George felt, he would use a good number of rhythmic, jittery figurations, reflecting the mood of the times.

It was 1924 and America was in the middle of a great boom and ferment. Business was great; it was as if nothing could go wrong. It was as if the country had suddenly come awake culturally, too. New writers and poets were turning out new books, and people were actually reading them. New ideas were being introduced almost every day—psychiatry, relativity—for even thinking had become an exciting adventure.

Why not music? Some of the "very rhythms of American life," as George termed them, could be set to music. He was extremely conscious of Americanism in music, of America of the time—the Jazz Age, as F. Scott Fitzgerald called it. George hoped to accomplish in music what writers like Fitzgerald and Hemingway accomplished in their books. "Music must reflect the

thoughts and aspirations of the people and the time,"
George said. "My people are American. My time is
today."

These were the thoughts that flitted through
George's mind when he returned to the Gershwin
apartment on 110th Street. It was a busy, bustling
household. Besides his parents, there were also Ira and
the teen-agers Arthur and Frances, whom everyone
called Frankie. She was a wonderful dancer and singer.
Mother Gershwin entertained her friends in the apartment, which was rarely quiet. Only Pop Gershwin
seemed to be in the background most of the time.

So that George could work in comparative isolation,
a room in the back of the apartment was set aside for
him. It was equipped with an upright piano and a
door, which was all George seemed to need. On January 7, 1924, he began composing his "American Rhapsody." Ira would visit him from time to time and they
would discuss the piece. After an afternoon spent in an
art gallery, Ira came by to hear how George was doing.
Colors were fresh in his mind as he listened to George
play the new composition.

"Why not," shyly suggested Ira, "call it *Rhapsody in
Blue?*"

George liked that better than his own title; he let-
tered it across the top of the first page of his manuscript. Because Ferde Grofé, Paul Whiteman's ar-
ranger, would do the orchestration George composed
for two pianos: one was the solo instrument, which he

would play, and the other represented the orchestra's part.

Whiteman's musicians were world-famous and naturally Grofé assigned them passages in the *Rhapsody* which would show what they could do. George, too, had many ideas—such as the opening clarinet whoop, an effect for which Ross Gorman had become a celebrity among musicians. This effect, more accurately called a *glissando* (in which a series of notes slid into one another), was considered impossible to play on the clarinet until Ross Gorman found a way to do it. The effect was electrifying.

For himself George composed some very prickly piano passages, showing what he could do as a pianist. All the other instruments were assigned special roles: the trumpet was given typically blaring jazz passages; the banjo supplied an almost quaint rhythmic emphasis; the clarinets decorated certain notes with the curlicue figures of the hot licks. To carry the romantic middle theme, there was a full complement of non-jazz strings: the violins, violas and cellos.

Day by day, page by page, the *Rhapsody in Blue* grew. Ferde would come around to the Gershwin apartment daily to pick up whatever George had completed the evening, and morning, before. In three weeks George completed the piano copy, except for a few piano flourishes he was confident he could improvise at the concert.

Rehearsals were held at the Palais Royale, where Whiteman's band was appearing at the time. In the deserted ballroom the band would assemble in the middle of the day to practice and to learn the new work. George played, Whiteman conducted and friends came to listen. The *Rhapsody in Blue* may have been a three-week creation, but all agreed that it "had something," even if they couldn't quite say what it was. It was brash, fresh, original—though obviously influenced by the Hungarian rhapsodies—and it did have an actual musical personality of its own. The "something" that the *Rhapsody in Blue* had was the touch of George Gershwin.

So it grew, through those few weeks between the announcement that Ira had found and the afternoon of the concert. It was, finally, more or less written out, more or less rehearsed, and more or less memorized.

George waited to go on. The orchestra had just completed a group of so-called "semiclassical" selections in dance tempo. The last of the three numbers was Rudolph Friml's *Chansonette* (later to be better known as "The Donkey Serenade"); the audience, now fairly bored, responded with less than enthusiastic applause.

It was time for George to go on.

The audience, by now, was in the mood where it dared you to make something happen. All the academic examples of so-called old jazz compared to the so-called new jazz had just about run its limit.

Something was happening onstage. The orchestra was enlarged, more strings were added, and a second piano was pushed out from the wings. A very young man—obviously the composer of the next piece, according to the program—hurried to the piano bench at the center of the stage. Whiteman quickly checked the band. They were ready. So was George, seated at the great ebony piano, looking like a boy. Whiteman gave the cue to Ross Gorman to begin the *Rhapsody in Blue.*

The audience sat straight up in their seats. The whooping *glissando* broke into an amusing cackle, the orchestra came in to exchange comments with the clarinet; soon after, George made his entrance, playing in his crisp, sure, manner. To many in the audience it seemed a miracle that this young man could play so well, let alone be the composer of this outrageous piece.

The audience was not aware of the fact that the entire work was not completely written out. Whiteman's conductor's score contained many blank pages where George was expected to play the piano passages. The score was very unusual; at some spots Grofé merely indicated the first name of a musician rather than the instrument.

George was now playing a very tricky solo. He could sense that the audience waited with electric expectancy, wondering what he would do next. George enjoyed that kind of attention.

On the podium Paul Whiteman knew that his "Experiment" was now a success. The *Rhapsody in Blue*—and George—were making American musical history. Whiteman was so overcome that he lost his place in the score. He found it after many blank pages. George was

enjoying himself with some flashy playing. Whiteman
almost burst out laughing, for there was his cue in the
score, certainly not what was taught in the musical
textbooks: "Wait for nod" was the simple instruction.

Completing his cadenza, George nodded to Paul,
who brought in the orchestra. The beautiful middle
theme (later to be Paul Whiteman's musical signature)
filled Aeolian Hall.

Not long after, the final chords of the *Rhapsody in
Blue* echoed through the auditorium. A breathless moment of silence followed, then came the thunderous
applause and the shouting.

Beaming, George stood beside the piano, acknowl-
edging the thrilling acceptance of his first concert
work. Paul came over to shake his hand. The sound of
applause reverberated through the hall; it was almost
deafening.

George bowed a little self-consciously and hurried to
the wings. There his friends congratulated him, em-
braced him, pounded him on the back. He had to go
out to take another bow. George was happy, not only
because of the success of the *Rhapsody*, but because he
knew that his parents were out there, and Ira, Arthur,
Frankie, relatives and friends. They were all certain
that their Georgie had invented American music. To
judge from the reception he was getting, maybe he
had.

Chapter 8

PRINCE GEORGE

Wednesday, February 13, 1924: George awakened to find himself among the famous. Until the Whiteman concert, George's fame was confined to the members of his family, a large circle of friends, and a number of musicians. Now the entire musical world was aware of him. So was the general public. He was only twenty-five, but George Gershwin was already being hailed as the hope of American music.

Not that the newspaper critics found every note of the *Rhapsody* to be pure gold. Some found fault with its at times inexpert handling of form; some didn't even like the idea of its use of jazz materials; others even hinted that George was a song composer who belonged in Tin Pan Alley, not in Aeolian Hall. But most agreed that it "added a new chapter to our musical history," whatever the technical shortcomings.

No one was more aware of the *Rhapsody*'s shortcomings than George. To begin with, he simply hadn't given it the time he wished he could have. He became more conscious of the lessons he had been skipping with Edward Kilenyi because writing songs for musicals left him little time for study.

George was aware, too, of the fact that much of the impact of the *Rhapsody in Blue* owed a great deal to Ferde Grofé's orchestration. George knew he must give more attention to the employment of instruments in the orchestra and to the form of concert works if he was to continue composing for the concert hall.

Meanwhile, he enjoyed his glory. The concert had created a great enough stir to be repeated again at Aeolian Hall in March and at Carnegie Hall in April. George was having a wonderful time.

He always had a good time when he was playing his own music. There were those who said he played his own music too much. At Van Vechten's parties, or the parties of Jules Glaenzer, George would take over at the piano and dominate the evening. If he brought a girl, she was forgotten in favor of his songs. Soon George would be surrounded by a group of admiring girls and, often as not, equally admiring concert pianists who found his playing fascinating.

George loved to play and he enjoyed his own music as much as his admiring audience. He regarded his own creations with the same loving detachment as a parent has for a beautiful and gifted child. Once a song had been given its final form and had taken on a personality and life of its own, George could admire it as much as anyone else. It was almost as if he hadn't written it.

This ability to view his work objectively was often mistaken for ego. Few people knew how many of his songs, treated to the same scrutiny, were discarded and never heard from again. George wanted people only to hear his best.

He was self-centered, of course. He was completely dedicated to music, and his music was George Gershwin. He practically lived no life apart from it. He liked sports, and particularly loved to play golf and tennis, but the time given to them was actually stolen from his real love. He wanted to know everything there was to know about music, its history, its technical side. He never stopped studying throughout his entire life. He gave much thought to finding teachers who could increase his knowledge. The only trouble was that, as his fame grew, fewer and fewer teachers were willing to take the celebrated Gershwin as a pupil. What, they asked, could they teach him?

Some of George's friends even tried to discourage his search for teachers and more formal study. They argued that it might spoil what natural talent he had. George argued that a talent that would be spoiled by study deserved to be spoiled. He went his own way as usual.

George had a great number of friends, though few close ones. Many were naturally connected with the music business, or were collaborators. As his reputation grew, so did the number of people who considered themselves his very dearest friends, or discoverers. Always gracious and polite, George did find it difficult to remember the names of everyone who greeted him familiarly with, "Hi, George!"

Among his closest friends were Emily and Lou Paley, who dated back to his years as a teen-age piano pounder. Lou was an English teacher who occasionally tried his hand at writing song lyrics; he had supplied George with a few as early as 1919. Lou was more devoted to teaching and his books than to song writing, however. His wife, Emily, was an extraordinarily lovely young girl who combined beauty with a sweetness of character and intelligence. George was very fond of both Paleys and remained close to them all his life.

Even before Emily and Lou were married, George frequently visited the Paley home on Sunday evenings. Lou's brother, Herman, himself a successful songwriter and like George a pupil of Charles Hambitzer, invited George to the Sunday night social evenings. Also attending these evenings were other young musicians, artists, writers—anyone, in fact, interested in the arts. The evenings were stimulating, often devoted to heated discussions and even arguments, for everyone was very young and excitable, most of them still in their teens.

George, even then, was often in the center of controversy. Some of the members of the Paley group were interested in "serious" music. They could not understand why the Paleys cultivated a "ragtime piano player" like George, who seemed more interested in popular music and jazz than the classics.

The arguments that resulted generally upset Emily, angered Lou and Herman, and didn't seem to bother George at all. He knew what he was planning to do and how he would do it. All the talk, as far as he was concerned, was merely talk.

George brought Ira to one of the Sunday evening sessions, for Ira could hold his own in the discussion of books and art much better than he. At the Paleys he met Leonore Strunsky, Emily's striking, vivacious sister, who would some years later become Mrs. Ira Gershwin.

Ira was so unlike George that it seemed they were opposite sides of the same Gershwin coin. Ira was by nature slow-moving, patient, careful, not given over to excitement. George always seemed to be in a rush, anxious to get to the next job, stirring things up wherever he went.

Both Ira and George shared the same attitude in their work, a serious concern with craftsmanship. No detail was so small that it didn't get attention. While their songs sparkled with an irreverent humor, they were fashioned with a serious skill. Ira could spend weeks polishing a single line of a lyric, although George could compose an entire song in an evening. But both words and music, once blended, fused into a single unit of perfection that came to be recognized as the Gershwin song.

George had worked with a number of good lyricists before Ira decided to take up song writing, but his finest work was done with his brother. They had not yet, as of February 13, 1924, hit their stride, but it was obvious that they soon would. For all the diversity of their personalities, professionally they were identical twins.

In 1924, Ira was still hidden behind a pen name he had concocted from the names of his younger brother and sister, "Arthur Francis." It seemed to him that the name of Gershwin was too celebrated in Tin Pan Alley for him to try to make his way under it. There were too many handicaps, such as being accused of trying to cash in on his kid brother's reputation, or being examined with more than normal criticism just because he was a Gershwin.

Ira believed that if he wanted to make his own way in the song writing business, he'd best do it without any "help" from the family name. He did, too. As Arthur Francis he collaborated with another fine composer, Vincent Youmans, on the successful show *Two Little Girls in Blue,* in 1921. The early songs he wrote with George were generally signed "Arthur Francis." Not until late in 1924 was Ira to come out from behind his disguise. And Ira did not become George's collaborator just because he happened to be handy; he was the best lyricist George knew.

Ira was also as much George's friend as he was his brother. Of all the members of the family, Ira understood best what it was that George was working toward.

Mom and Pop Gershwin were very proud of George, they were happy that he was successful, but his work was always to remain a bit of a mystery to them, especially the concert pieces. George was fortunate in having Ira close at hand to discuss his problems with and to talk about art and music in general.

One of George's closest friends was William Daly, a former magazine editor turned musician. Bill Daly was George's favorite conductor. Bill was a sensitive, understanding musician who, like Ira, understood George's musical ideas and respected George's musicianship.

Besides the few close friends, George's circle included hundreds of acquaintances, people he had met at parties, people who had made a point of meeting him, people he had never met but who wanted to meet him, and people who worshiped celebrities.

George was regularly invited to the homes of society folk who dabbled in the arts and who liked to display a social daring by having popular composers on hand to play the latest songs of the day. George was always in demand, not only because he didn't have to be coaxed to the piano where he performed brilliantly, but also because, since the Whiteman concert, he had become the notorious composer of "serious jazz music."

Essentially, George Gershwin was a very lonely young man. He drove himself in his work to the point where he seemed to feel no need of another person. When he was completely alone, he found solace in his music. Nevertheless he was rarely ever allowed really to be alone. Friends and acquaintances were dropping by all the time. The miracle was that he ever got anything done. But he needed the companionship, he liked the hubbub, the tingle of excitement, the obvious pleasure that people found in his music. The moments when there was no music, no admiring crowds— those were bitter. George could only bury those moments with activity.

He was very busy in the spring of 1924, following the great splash of the *Rhapsody in Blue*. There was a *Scandals* score to write; his last one, as it turned out, for George White. George had become tired of the production-line kind of composing he did for the *Scandals*. That last *Scandals*, however, was graced with one of his most memorable songs, "Somebody Loves Me."

He was invited to London to write a musical titled *Primrose*, which proved to be so great a hit that it erased the memory of the year before. George had traveled to London then, too, but the show, a revue titled *Rainbow*, proved to be a disaster. George, at the time, had felt lucky to have been able to get out of England. The round-trip ticket had proved a wise purchase.

Primrose was most successful. So successful, in fact, that the publisher was encouraged to publish its complete "vocal score," all of the music and lyrics in a book. It was the first of George's scores to be published in full. It was also the first musical for which he wrote some of the orchestrations. Only three numbers, but it gave him practice. The next time he was commissioned to write a concert piece, he was determined that it would be an all-Gershwin job.

When he returned to New York it was to start work on another show for his old friend Alex Aarons, who had produced *La La Lucille.* Alex had formed a producing partnership with Vinton Freedley, a onetime actor. They decided that they would try to produce unpretentious yet tasteful shows that would be more sophisticated than the usual show of the Twenties. The show they had in mind for George was *Black-Eyed Susan,* which would star the now internationally famous dance team, Fred and Adele Astaire. Ira was to do the lyrics—and as Ira Gershwin; "Arthur Francis" could retire. It was practically a family affair.

The year 1924 closed as it had begun for George, in a blaze of glory. By the time it had opened on Broadway in December, *Black-Eyed Susan* had become *Lady, Be Good,* one of the great hit shows of the Twenties. It was George and Ira's first major success.

The show's title was changed as soon as the producers heard a song George and Ira called "Oh, Lady Be Good!" The other songs were equally sophisticated; they were literate and musically miles above the average song. Typical was the intricate "Fascinating Rhythm" which George had begun in London and completed in New York. Its very fascinating rhythms presented Ira with difficult word problems which he managed with characteristic skill. One of their best songs, however,

was cut from the show because it was thought that it
held it up. The song was "The Man I Love," which was
destined to be cut from at least three other shows yet
was to become one of the most popular of all Gershwin
creations and one of the outstanding songs of American popular music.

The Gershwins' next show, however, which opened
early in 1925 served to remind George that his path
would not always be strewn with hits. *Tell Me More*
closed after only 32 performances. But like "The Man
I Love," it took a typical Gershwin turn of fate; when
it opened in London a month later *Tell Me More* was
a hit!

Something even more important happened to
George. He had been commissioned by the New York
Symphony Society (which later merged with the New
York Philharmonic) to compose a piano concerto. Walter Damrosch had been in the Aeolian Hall audience
when George played the *Rhapsody in Blue* and had
made up his mind that he would have a Gershwin composition for his orchestra. George very happily signed
a contract for the concerto which he would introduce
with the Society orchestra, playing seven concerts in
four cities—New York, Washington, Philadelphia and
Baltimore.

After signing the contract, George went out and
bought a book to find out exactly what a piano concerto was.

Chapter 9

"... A COMPOSITION FOR
A SOLO PLAYER
AND AN ORCHESTRA ..."

Gᴇᴏʀɢᴇ knew, of course, what a concerto was. He had heard dozens of them in the concert halls, but he did realize that his textbook knowledge of the formal, classic concerto was sketchy. His theoretical studies had been more concerned with musical sound, with harmony, and not so much with the form, or "structure," of a musical work. George had enjoyed analyzing what Bach did with his theme, the main melodic idea, in the great *Art of the Fugue*. It was treated to various manipulations: it was to be played slow, or fast; higher or lower, or backward—there seemed to be no end to what could be done with a musical idea, and Bach's rich imagination. But a concerto was not limited to a single theme, but several.

Also, George knew that composing for the New York Symphony Society Orchestra was not the same as writing for the Paul Whiteman band. George wanted to know more about orchestration, the handling of the different instruments in a great orchestra. He bought a book on orchestration, too. But most of all, he must know more about the concerto form—he couldn't just string out a series of musical ideas, as he had in the *Rhapsody in Blue,* and hope to be lucky again.

George knew very well that a concerto was "a composition for a solo player and an orchestra." It was divided into three sections called "movements." The word concerto derived from the Latin *concertare* which means "to compete side by side," in other words a combination of competition and cooperation.

The idea of the concerto was based upon the classic sonata form as it was developed by Bach's sons, and Haydn, Mozart and Beethoven. Its basic form was one based upon the dramatic contrasts in tempo—Allegro-Adagio-Allegro (Fast-Slow-Fast)—but within this broad outline, George learned as he studied other concertos, there was a great deal of room for the composer to let his own imagination run freely. His major problem was to take the standard concerto form, work within it without doing its traditions undue violence, and yet express his own musical personality.

When he was in London in June 1925, for the rehearsals and opening of *Tell Me More,* George began sketching out ideas for a work he was planning to title

"New York Concerto." From its very beginning his concerto was to be different. Having studied the book definition of the concerto, its correct structure, George decided that he would write a work that reflected the feel of a great city. While it would not tell a story, it would represent his feelings about New York in 1925; this was George's idea of a piano concerto, not the book's.

By July George was back in New York at work on the concerto. He had bought a five-story house at 316 West 103rd Street, just off Riverside Drive. Gershwins were distributed throughout the first four floors; the fifth was reserved for George. The Gershwin house, however, did not always give George the privacy he sometimes needed. His and Ira's friends were always dropping by. So were Arthur's and Frankie's. Mama Gershwin's girl friends found it a good place for their weekly card parties. Pop Gershwin, as usual, stayed in the background, though he found the new self-service elevator fascinating. Some visitors even mistook him for an elevator operator.

Often the house was overrun by family friends that neither George nor Ira knew. As the summer drew on, George's problem grew bigger: not only was he to work on the concerto which was scheduled to be premiered in early December, he also had to collaborate with Ira on a musical, *Tip Toes,* for Aarons and Freedley, and with Oscar Hammerstein II and Otto Harbach on *Song of the Flame,* another musical. Both musicals were also slated for December premieres.

To get away from the far-from-private house, George would escape to a nearby hotel where he had rented a room and had a piano put into it. He managed to get some work done until friends discovered where he was and invaded the room.

Ernest Hutcheson, a good friend and fine piano teacher, came to the rescue for a while. Hutcheson was teaching during the summer at Chautauqua, in New York State. He had a small hut reserved for George in the musical colony where he could work without interruption. The orders to Hutcheson's students were that they were not to disturb George until late in the afternoon. They followed orders, but rarely failed to come around about four to hear George play.

In spite of all the activity that seemed to center about him, George completed the piano sketch of the concerto's first movement that hectic July. The second movement took him all of August and part of September; the remaining weeks of September were spent on the final movement.

October and November were devoted, between conferences and rehearsals of the two musicals, to orchestrating the concerto. On November 10, 1925, George completed his piano concerto. He no longer called it the "New York Concerto"; it was now simply and very classically titled *Concerto in F for Piano and Orchestra.*

Two weeks before the official rehearsals under Walter Damrosch were to take place, George took over the Globe Theatre one afternoon, hired an orchestra and with Bill Daly conducting, and himself at the piano, was able to get a good idea of how the *Concerto in F* would sound in actual performance. In the almost deserted theatre were Ira, Walter Damrosch, four music critics, and the usual group of friends. It was an unusual way to test a new musical work, but George could afford it and he was anxious to have it sounding right before the official rehearsals. As a result of this run-through, George made about a half dozen changes.

The *Concerto in F* was ready for its first public performance the afternoon of December 3, 1925. It was a cold, wet, blustery winter day, but Carnegie Hall was filled. George Gershwin was good box office.

He was almost late for this important event because he dallied in a warm tub too long. No composer's stomach that day. Luckily, however, his friend the composer Phil Charig came around to get George on his way. It was, of course, a gala Gershwin afternoon. George was in excellent form and played in his usual crisp yet romantic style. Perhaps the orchestra encountered some spots in the concerto that proved a bit too jazzy for their tastes, but all seemed to have a good time, including the audience. The critics, as usual, were a little mystified and therefore extra critical.

As with the *Rhapsody in Blue,* the convention-bound critics found the concerto "weak in structure," and less striking than the earlier work (that is, it did not use a dance band). No one, however, questioned the originality and ingenuity of George's invention as found in the opening in which the kettledrums boomed and the orchestra broke into a Charleston. George's major piano theme was recognized as one of his finest creations. It was remarkably simple, too. The orchestra had been booming and Charlestoning when, in a comparatively peaceful moment, the piano announced its presence, then slipped, via the *glissando*, one of George's favorite devices throughout the concerto, into the theme proper. It was an ingenious working of just a few notes, but it was most effective. Under the piano's playing could be heard typical Gershwin harmonies that George had assigned to the English horn and violas. It was a lovely effect.

The middle movement was beautifully poetic, a night piece in which, again over enchanting harmonies, a typical Gershwin blues was played by a muted trumpet. The piano entered to treat the blues in a crackling, almost satirical manner.

The last movement bristled with rhythm and served to close the concerto with a nervous, bustling, New York-ish excitement.

George Gershwin had succeeded in composing a real piano concerto and, even if all the critics were not happy with it, the audience had been. One critic even suggested that George had not done the orchestration —in its way, a kind of compliment.

George thought of the concerto as his "most serious work," which it was up to that time. It was to remain, throughout his life, his most important orchestral composition, one for which he had a special fondness. Many now regard it the first important work in concerto form composed by an American; some, indeed, still regard it as the outstanding American piano concerto.

In the *Concerto in F* George took a giant step forward from the *Rhapsody in Blue*. He proved, to begin with, that he was no mere flash in the pan. He proved that he could work within the limitations of classic forms without limiting his own invention. His musical personality did not always lend itself to rules, for George composed out of a natural urge to make music, an urge that could not be bound by rules.

A writer once called Gershwin "the happiest singer of his generation," and it was true—George was at his best when he was singing, for his richest gift was his ability for melodic invention, whether of concerto themes or popular songs.

The musical ideas in the *Concerto in F* are pure Gershwin; the orchestration—all Gershwin, too—did not depend upon the shocking effects of a jazz band for its impact, yet George managed to use touches that were daringly jazzy—the Charleston motif in the first movement, the blues trumpet in the second, the many blue notes throughout and the jazzy—or rather, typical —Gershwinisms in the solo piano part.

George had succeeded in bringing Tin Pan Alley, a touch of New Orleans, Broadway and, most importantly, Gershwin to Carnegie Hall.

Chapter 10

AMERICANS IN PARIS

Unlike many other American artists of the Twenties, George never had the urge to leave the United States in order "to find himself" artistically. In America, and especially in New York, he found all the inspiration he needed. His music was in demand; the *Rhapsody in Blue* and the *Concerto in F* were being regularly performed and there were requests for new concert works. George and Ira could do at least two show scores a year, if they felt so inclined, and many of their songs were pleasantly popular.

The New York scene, the theatre, the parties—all these were stimulating to George. But by the spring of 1928 he felt it was time to get a little time off.

Since the premiere of the *Concerto in F* he and Ira had been extremely busy turning out shows, most of them successes, a few not. George had had time only in that period to compose a suite of *Piano Preludes*. In the back of his mind he had the idea that he would like to try his hand at composing an opera. To tackle such a job George felt he should take the time out from writing the musical comedy songs, which had made him a wealthy young man, to study.

So he and Ira decided that they would take a few months during the spring of 1928 to visit Europe. They would take with them Ira's wife, Leonore, and their sister Frankie. It would be a real holiday after many years of concentrated work. Besides, George hoped that he might be able to study with some great European teacher such as Nadia Boulanger, who had been the teacher of the American composers Aaron Copland, Virgil Thomson and Roy Harris. Ira was interested in seeing Paris the city of the American expatriates—Ernest Hemingway, Ezra Pound and the other members of the Gertrude Stein circle. They would see all the museums and the sights.

Besides all this, George had a commission from the New York Symphony Society for a composition for orchestra which he hoped to work on between sightseeing jaunts. It was typical of him to work even when he seemed to be getting away from work.

Five days before the Gershwin party was to embark for London, George had a taste of what was in store for him. The great French composer Maurice Ravel, a friend also of Eva Gauthier, was in New York after a tour of the United States. March 7, 1928, was to be

his fifty-third birthday. Mme. Gauthier planned to
have a party in celebration of the event. When she
asked Ravel what he wanted most of all, the French
musician informed her that he wanted to meet and
hear George Gershwin.

George and Ravel met in an atmosphere of mutual
admiration, although it was George who presided at
the piano, for Ravel was fascinated by his playing as
well as his music. George played the entire *Rhapsody
in Blue* for Ravel, and dozens of songs. The tricks that
George did with rhythms particularly delighted Ravel.
It was a warm and friendly meeting—and George could
not let the opportunity slip by. Through Mme.
Gauthier, George asked Ravel if he might become his
pupil.

Mme. Gauthier translated Ravel's reply: "Why be a
second-rate Ravel when you are already a first-rate
Gershwin?" If Gershwin was to study with him, Ravel
believed that George would lose his originality of style.
George's style was wonderful just as it was, said Ravel;
no, he would not be his teacher. This was a fine compliment from so great a musician, but it did not solve
George's problem. Perhaps when they got to Europe . . .

In London they attended the opening of a show of
Ira's, with music by Phil Charig, titled *That's a Good
Girl,* which began their travels on a happy note. By the
end of March they had settled in Paris for a three
months' stay. From Paris they were able to visit other

European cities, such as Vienna, home of the operetta.

Paris was much like New York for George. There was a continual round of parties at which he held forth at the piano. He met many famous musicians—Stravinsky, Poulenc, Prokofiev, Milhaud and, of course, Ravel again. And it seemed that everywhere they went they encountered Gershwin music: there was the *Rhapsody in Blue* at the Théâtre Mogador and the *Concerto in F,* in its European premiere, at the Théâtre National de l'Opéra. At the Champs-Elysées Theatre they even watched the Ballet Russe dance to the *Rhapsody.*

As for Frankie, Cole Porter worked her into the show at Les Ambassadeurs, where she sang Gershwin songs in a manner that always pleased George.

Whenever he could, between meetings with composers and musicians, or talking to newspapermen, George worked at his new composition in his suite at the Hôtel Majestic. He had decided, before they had left New York, that he would write a piece about Paris, something he had wanted to do since his first short visit there in 1923. It was in Paris that he composed a very appealing blues in which he attempted to express the homesickness of an American in Paris. As in New York, George played the piece for anyone who dropped in, and there was a steady stream of visitors, among them the conductor Leopold Stokowski, the English composer William Walton, Vladimir Dukelsky, a young Russian composer of serious music who

wanted to write popular songs (as Vernon Duke, a
name devised for him by George, he became a well-
known songwriter of such excellent songs as "April in
Paris" and "I Can't Get Started"; the last with lyrics
by Ira).

For George, it was as if he had never left home.

He was not successful in becoming anyone's pupil,
either. The great musicians, who had such a fine time
listening to him play and delighted in his songs, were
astonished by his request. Their next action was to
refuse him. Even Nadia Boulanger, who preferred
teaching to composing, felt there was nothing she
could teach George; his gift was fine the way it was.
Meanwhile . . .

". . . would you play that 'Fascinating Rhythm'
again?"

". . . or 'Fidgety Feet'?"

". . . 'Do Do Do'?"

". . . 'Looking For a Boy'? There is a lovely
melody, so like Brahms!"

"And your new work, Mr. Gershwin—the one with
that blues melody—would you play that? What do you
call it?"

"An American in Paris."

It was time to get back home. There were cable-
grams from producers with offers to do new shows.
The New York Times reported that George's new
composition, although still far from completed, was
scheduled to be played by the Philharmonic.

London and Vienna and Paris had been exciting, but George was homesick—for there is no doubting that the American portrayed in *An American in Paris* is George Gershwin.

Chapter 11

MUSIC MAKING — GERSHWIN STYLE

In 1928 home to both George and Ira was the twin penthouses atop the tall apartment house at 33 Riverside Drive on West 75th Street. George lived in one penthouse and Lee and Ira in the other. Whenever the brothers wanted to work, it was a simple matter to step across the terrace.

The view was like a movie backdrop, with Manhattan spreading out for miles below; to the west was the Hudson River and New Jersey. George's apartment was very modern with severe geometric furniture, tables and bookcases. The grand piano added a graceful touch in ebony. The walls of both apartments were covered with paintings by contemporary artists, for both George and Ira admired and collected modern art. George's bookcases were stocked with books on music and bound scores by various composers, favorites of George's, from Bach to Stravinsky. In the corner of one room there was an unusual, and yet typical, touch: a punching bag projected from the wall and near it a pair of boxing gloves, for George liked to keep in trim by punching the bag whenever he couldn't get out for tennis or golf. On the floor was a rowing machine and, for less strenuous exertion, a dart board.

Usually George did his composing at night, after everyone else had gone to bed and even the city seemed to be resting quietly as it glittered around him. After a night of work George would be up around noon; if he had no appointments for the day he spent the afternoon making orchestrations or piano copies of songs set down the night before. As he played them over with a critical ear cocked, perhaps a couple no longer sounded as good to him as they had then and they were discarded.

In the early evening George might go to a party at Van Vechten's, or Jules Glaenzer's, or the publisher Condé Nast's. Or he might go to the theatre or visit friends. At the parties, as he played, George might strike upon a melodic phrase or a rhythmic figure that interested him. Often as not he developed the idea into a song at the party, or would jot it down for work when he returned to his apartment.

Because he almost always composed the music before Ira did the words, George worked alone in his apartment. When the time came to put the songs into a

show, the brothers worked long hours together fitting
and polishing the words and music into a perfect unit.

"I can think of no more nerve-racking, no more
mentally arduous task than music making," George
once said. "There are times when a phrase of music
will cost many hours of internal sweating. Rhythms
romp through one's brain, but they're not easy to capture and keep . . ."

George preferred to work during the winter months,
for if the weather was pleasant he found he'd rather be
out of doors. But when he had to, he worked hard and
long, often as not with a cigar in his mouth. He would
seat himself at the piano, light the cigar, and begin
searching the keyboard for ideas.

"Composing at the piano," he said, "is not a good
practice. But I started that way and it has become a
habit." George believed that even the sound of the
piano interfered with the free play of the musical imagination. "The actual composition," he explained,
"must be done in the brain.

"Too much, however, should not be left to the memory. Sometimes, after the phrase seems safe in the
mind, it will be lost by the next day. When I get a
phrase which I am not sure I will remember the following day I set it down on paper at once."

That mysterious element of inspiration, so roman-
ticized in novels and especially movies, played little
part in George Gershwin's composition. Of his yearly
output of songs, which probably numbered well into

the hundreds, he once said that "perhaps two—or at the most, three—come as a result of inspiration."

As for songs coming in the middle of the night, George had this to say: "Occasionally compositions come in dreams, but rarely can they be remembered when you wake. On one occasion I did get out of bed to write a song." (It was the comic march, "Strike Up the Band.")

But George felt, "We can never rely on inspiration. Making music is actually little else than a matter of invention aided and abetted by emotion. In composing we combine what we know with what we feel." In his work George always hoped to keep the two in balance; he wanted to give equal attention in his work to what he called "the head and the heart," a balance of the emotional with the intellectual.

The Gershwin party returned from Europe late in June, 1928. George immediately got out his paper, pencils and cigars and gave his attention to *An American in Paris*. He completed the piano sketch by the first of August. Unlike the *Rhapsody* and *Concerto,* the *American* did not require a piano soloist; it was an orchestral work which George called a "rhapsodic ballet." As he worked on the concert work George, characteristically, collaborated with Ira on *Treasure Girl,* a musical.

Treasure Girl opened on November 8th; George completed the orchestration of *An American in Paris* ten days later. It was ready for Walter Damrosch and the Philharmonic.

George was in high spirits the afternoon of December 13th, the day of the concert. As he walked along 57th Street with a group of friends he demonstrated some tricky new dance steps. After this his shoes required touching up, for which the shoeshine boy received five dollars. George was regarded as a very good dancer with an unusual sense of rhythm; he often illustrated the rhythms of his songs by dancing to them. His imitation of Fred Astaire was nimble and almost uncanny.

Once inside Carnegie Hall, the Gershwin group listened to *An American in Paris*. It proved to be a charming and popular composition. George began it imaginatively with the saucy and jaunty "walking themes" introducing the American walking through the streets of Paris. "My purpose here is to portray the impression of an American visitor in Paris, as he strolls about the city and listens to various street noises and absorbs French atmosphere."

George literally brought the street noises into Carnegie Hall by using French taxi horns as instruments in the orchestra. When he had been in Paris and himself strolling about the city, George came across a shop where he bought a set of horns. Even if the listener's imagination did not supply the impressions of Paris, George's walking themes, the bustling orchestra and the taxi horns did it all very vividly. The blues section, which he had composed in Paris, followed the walking themes, but once the homesickness had passed, the American's high spirits returned to more lively, very

Parisian music. The street noises return to close the work on a happy note.

In *An American in Paris* George proved himself an even more skilled orchestrator than he was in the *Concerto in F*. It was very well received and George was happy at the usual parties that followed the premiere. At one he was presented with a fine silver cigar humidor on which the signatures of dozens of friends had been inscribed.

But *An American in Paris* was more than his latest concert work; it was to become the one that furnished him with yet another outlet for what seemed to be unlimited talents. In August of 1929 George made his debut as a conductor at Lewisohn Stadium. *The New York Times,* in reporting this new Gershwin first, noted that George "could hardly contain his enthusiasm." It was not noticeable that he had never lead an orchestra before. To prepare for this important debut George simply practiced at home by placing the recording of *An American in Paris* on the phonograph, cranking up, and conducting away.

The previous February his friend Nat Shilkret had recorded the complete *American* for RCA Victor. George had taken part in the recording, though it was rather accidental. He was also "enthusiastic" at the recording session, so much so that he sometimes got into Shilkret's way during the rehearsal. Shilkret asked George to leave at least until the orchestra was properly rehearsed. A bit hurt, George managed to stay away for a little while, and quickly forgot his wounded ego when he heard what Shilkret had accomplished.

During the rehearsal Shilkret discovered that he had not been informed that, while there was no piano in the score, it did call for a celesta (a small pianolike instrument that makes a sweet tinkling sound). So he drafted George for the job.

It was this recording that George used to practice his conducting; about every 4½ minutes he would have to stop to turn the record over, but that didn't dampen his enthusiasm.

At the concert he led the orchestra as if the work had never been played before. He cued in the musicians with remarkable precision, he encouraged them to make the romantic passages lyrical, the dramatic passages climactic, the percussive passages sharp and almost theatrical. The audience had as good a time as George. He was rewarded with several rounds of enthusiastic applause, which he graciously shared with the orchestra by asking them to stand. George decided he really found conducting to be fun, he would do more of it.

The following November he conducted the *American* again to the same reception he had received at the Stadium. When his and Ira's show *Strike Up the Band* opened in Boston on Christmas Day, 1929, George conducted his first musical. When the show opened in New York on January 14, 1930, there was George again on the podium; one reviewer noted that the composer-conductor wore the world's largest white tie, with a gardenia to match.

After all this exertion George left in February for

Florida and a rest. He returned in April to sign a contract to do a movie score with Ira. The motion picture had only recently learned to talk and Hollywood was taking advantage of the novelty of sound by grinding out film musicals. With all of the best of Broadway's composers going out to Hollywood, it was natural that George and Ira would be asked to do a score also.

Before they could leave, however, George had other jobs to attend to: in May he appeared for a week at the Roxy Theatre with Paul Whiteman, in August he was again at Lewisohn Stadium as piano soloist and, of course, conductor. The rest of the summer and the days until mid-October were spent in preparing a musical comedy, *Girl Crazy*, for its opening.

The day after, George wrote to a friend, "I am just recuperating from a couple of very exciting days. I worked very hard conducting the orchestra at the rehearsal and dress rehearsal and finally at the opening night, when the theatre was so warm that I must have lost at least three pounds, perspiring. The opening was so well received that five pounds would not have been too much."

With *Girl Crazy* a hit, the Gershwins felt they could leave for Hollywood. *Strike Up the Band* was also still running; with two successes in a single year the Gershwins were welcome, indeed, in Hollywood, the land of success.

George was rather disappointed in Hollywood. The slow pace of the film center came as a decided letdown after his usual round of activity. Instead of the cus-

tomary dozen or more songs he had to write for a
Broadway musical, he found that the film required less
than half that number. Also, he and Ira were rarely
consulted as they always were during the making of a
Broadway show. They turned in their songs, which the
studio people always liked, but George and Ira never
knew how the songs would be used—if they were to be
used at all. Working in Hollywood was much different
from working in New York.

George, at least, found a release for his pent-up creative energies by composing some instrumental music
for the film which was titled *Delicious* and starred
Janet Gaynor and Charles Farrell.

The setting was New York City, so for the opening
of the film George composed what he called at first a
"Manhattan Rhapsody," and later titled "Rhapsody in
Rivets." The piano theme which began the rhapsody
was hammered out on a single note in a machinelike
manner which, to George, sounded like a riveting machine. This work, at least, gave him a great deal of
pleasure and kept him occupied. For the rest of the
Delicious score he dug into his notebooks for the half
dozen required songs.

The rest of the time he spent hiking in the Hollywood hills and canyons; he golfed, played tennis, swam
in the ever-present pools and went to what seemed an
endless round of parties. The phone rang so much that
George finally had it disconnected. He was then able to
work on his "Rhapsody in Rivets," which he had decided he would expand from the few minutes needed

for *Delicious* to a full-length work for piano and orchestra. In between, he and Ira began working on their next Broadway musical due to open at the end of the year.

Back in their respective penthouses early in 1931, Ira concentrated on inventing and polishing lyrics for the new show and George worked on his new rhapsody. By May 23rd he finished the entire work, including the orchestration. He had by then changed the title to *Second Rhapsody.* Though it has never become as popular as the *Rhapsody in Blue,* the *Second Rhapsody* is one of Gershwin's most interesting compositions. Not as romantic as the earlier work, the *Second Rhapsody* was regarded by George as "the best thing I've written" as far as orchestration and form were concerned. If the *Rhapsody in Blue* could conjure up colors, such as blue and at times purple, the *Second Rhapsody* must be thought of as stark black and white.

To study the work, George arranged for an orchestra to play in the studios of the National Broadcasting Company. During the rehearsal, which George conducted—he was also piano soloist—a recording was made so that he could study the effect of his orchestration as it actually sounded.

He barely had time to do all this when he found himself and Ira deep in their work on their new show, *Of Thee I Sing.* They had fun writing it, for like the earlier *Strike Up the Band,* it was a most unusual show. Because it was not a typical musical comedy, George and Ira had a chance to show what they could really do. They were not restricted to the conventional songs of the conventional show—the ballads, the rhythm numbers, the "openers," etc. Instead they could compose songs directly related to the show's plot.

They were working hard and enjoying themselves and they had no idea that they were producing one of the historic musicals of the American theatre.

Chapter 12

POLITICS AND
POPULAR SONG

THE Gershwin venture into musical politics began with the 1927 version of *Strike Up the Band*, which despite its brilliant book by George S. Kaufman failed to get to New York.

Kaufman's book, though disguised as feathery-brained musical comedy, was actually a pretty clear-and hard-eyed look at war. Possibly the bitterness of the book revealed too much of the pointless folly of man, the warrior. Even the sprightly music of George and the lighthearted lyrics of Ira did not lessen the sting of Kaufman's arrows. In almost so many words Kaufman said: "How foolish are our wars, how stupidly are they begun, and how eager are some to take full advantage of their misery and suffering."

But in 1927, when the Coolidge prosperity was at its peak, the stock market was booming and all was well, Americans were not very interested in seeing a show that seemed to carry a message. As for Europe— all they wanted to hear about that place was that a young aviator by the name of Lindbergh had flown there: nonstop, New York to Paris!

Besides, there were the more simple-minded, completely entertaining musicals to see. There was the Gershwins' own *Funny Face,* starring the Astaires, there was Vincent Youmans' *Hit the Deck,* or DeSylva, Brown and Henderson's *Good News,* and Rodgers and Hart's *A Connecticut Yankee.* The last musical had a book and the songs were more or less related to the plot, as they were in the romantic *Show Boat,* with songs by Jerome Kern and Oscar Hammerstein II. If the musical comedy-going American in 1927 wanted to see a show that taxed his mind a little with a story, he could see *A Connecticut Yankee* or *Show Boat.* But why see a musical that reminded him of war? The less said about that the better. *Strike Up the Band* had to close down in Philadelphia.

The producer Edgar Selwyn never lost faith in it, however. When the Gershwins were on their European tour the following year, Selwyn wrote them in Paris telling them that he planned to give the antiwar musical another try: would they be willing to risk more work on it?

Kaufman's book was rewritten by Morrie Ryskind, who removed many of the barbs and made the show easier for the general public to take (the critics had admired the '27 version very much). He succeeded in popularizing it at the expense of tampering with Kaufman's more honest point of view. What had once been criticism was changed to song and dance entertainment.

Despite the changes *Strike Up the Band* was still a satire on war, which in itself was a historic departure for musical comedy. It did have a book that actually made sense and it did present George and Ira with the chance to work on a real book show again.

This meant quite a lot of work for them, for about half of the songs from the original went out, among them such Gershwin gems as the sweet and naïve "Seventeen and Twenty-one," the satiric "Oh, This Is Such a Charming War," as well as "The Man I Love," which was fated never to stay in a musical. Among the new songs were the lovely ballad "Soon," the mocking "I Want to Be a War Bride," and "I've Got a Crush On You." The title song, which had come to George in his sleep, was used in both versions.

If the new *Strike Up the Band* pleased audiences in 1930, when the second version opened in New York, it pleased the Gershwins even more. At last they had been given the opportunity to write a show that was not just a series of numbers specially devised for a singer, a dancer or a comedian. Despite the revisions *Strike Up the Band* was no mere formula musical. In it George could use music as Ira used words, to underline the story or to help depict the personalities of the characters. He was able to display his gift for dramatic writing which tended to be overlooked in the conventional show. The songs had a definite personality, quality, and served to move the story along. This had never been a secret, but it took a show like *Strike Up the Band* to make it obvious.

As for Ira's lyrics, they were equal to George's music. The words were, if anything, even more important to the story. Not only did the lyrics become part of the book itself, they were so skillfully fashioned that they became a special kind of poetry.

George was very happy with the show. The opening night in New York, when he made his debut as a musical comedy conductor, he enjoyed himself so much whistling, singing and humming that one critic called him the star of the show. Once the show was running as a hit, he went back often to enjoy his and Ira's handiwork. Here was the kind of a musical he had been searching for; so was the American public, he felt.

"The American world is looking for a new style of musical comedy," he declared in 1930. The Twenties had come to a sad end with the great crash of the stock market; the depression brought the joyride of the Jazz Age to a sudden stop. The entertainments of that Era of Wonderful Nonsense no longer entertained, something new had to be found.

Part of the something new came with the production of the so-called "intimate revues" of the early Thirties. These were simply (which means inexpensively) but smartly produced shows that commented upon what was going on in the world, and the country, at the time. While there were good songs in these revues, there was also an undercurrent of satire aimed at the political scene, or politicians and current events in the United States.

Among the outstanding revues of this type were such shows as *Fine and Dandy* with a score by George's friend Kay Swift, the finest of America's lady song-writers. Another friend, Arthur Schwartz, wrote the songs for *The Little Shows* and *Three's a Crowd.* In 1932, Irving Berlin and Moss Hart actually took notice of the depression in the excellent and aptly titled *Face the Music.* The striking thing about all of these revues was the unusual element of intelligence and real wit, so clearly lacking in most of the Twenties' musicals.

Strike Up the Band had prepared the way. When, late in 1930, another producer, Sam H. Harris, asked George and Ira to write the score for another political show, book once more by Kaufman and Ryskind, they jumped at the chance.

The result was *Of Thee I Sing.*

This musical or, as the Gershwins generally called it, "political operetta," is one of the most important ever produced. It was historic, for it had many firsts connected with it. *Of Thee I Sing* was probably the first fully "integrated" musical—that is, every note of the music and every word of the lyrics were part of the plot. Every song in the score was designed especially for the show; there was no attempt, as there always was in the conventional musical, to insert individual numbers that could easily be taken out and made into hit songs.

Of Thee I Sing was the first musical to take as its subject the contemporary political scene. It poked fun at the presidency, and particularly at the vice-presidency; it drubbed the political parties, it mocked foreign relations and even found the Supreme Court a target for its sharp arrows. But it was all done with such good humor that few were angered by the satire.

As a result of its potshots, *Of Thee I Sing* was chosen the Pulitzer Prize play of the year—the first musical ever to be so honored.

Of Thee I Sing, even more than *Strike Up the Band,* changed the history of musical comedy in America. It was followed by shows that took American politics as their theme, that integrated songs with plot and that paid more attention to the book. After *Of Thee I Sing* it was difficult to produce any old musical comedy by throwing a few people and a few songs together.

In their score the Gershwins all but abandoned the use of the conventional "verse and chorus" songs. Instead there were such creations as "Wintergreen For President," which though very catchy was certainly no popular song. "Of Thee I Sing, Baby" came closer, but though supposedly a love song—a ballad—it did not take itself seriously enough to be a real ballad. Ira's lyrics, in fact, let the hot air out of the standard love song. So did "Who Cares?" with its reference to banks failing in Yonkers. Whoever put banks, and failing ones, into a so-called love song? Ira Gershwin did, and the audiences loved it, for the songs were perfectly in key with the spirit of the show.

One of the ingenious inventions of Kaufman and Ryskind was the character of Throttlebottom, the vice-president. During the past decade in American history the vice-president had been practically unknown. Some people didn't even know who he was or what he did. As portrayed by Victor Moore in *Of Thee I Sing,* one of the classic performances of the American theatre, the vice-president was a bumbling little man, meek and so undistinguished that he couldn't even get a library card in Washington because no one could recognize him. Some politicians, however, were not very happy with the way they were presented, as not very bright thieves. No one had the nerve to raise any objections for fear such an objection would be an admission of guilt. Besides it was only a musical comedy, and meant in good fun, for all the discomfort to some people.

The "American world" had found the show it was looking for: *Of Thee I Sing* was a smash hit and went on to enjoy the longest run of any Gershwin musical.

One of the shortest was that of *Let 'Em Eat Cake,* the sequel to *Of Thee I Sing.* Kaufman and Ryskind took the same characters of the earlier operetta, the president Wintergreen (Willam Gaxton) vice-president Throttlebottom (Victor Moore). Happily elected in *Of Thee I Sing,* the two are turned out of office as *Let 'Em Eat Cake* began. They regain their old jobs by staging a revolution. It was a nightmarish picture of an America that might have been, and the theatre audiences of

1933 didn't want any of it. The stories in the newspapers of European dictatorships was more than enough.

One critic did find *Let 'Em Eat Cake* a "funnier and crueler conspiracy against Washington, D. C." than *Of Thee I Sing* had been. But to many people the depression was conspiracy enough. Everyone naturally compared the two shows and it seemed that *Of Thee I Sing* was kinder in its satire, more full of fun, less biting.

Actually *Let 'Em Eat Cake* was ahead of its time. The tough realism of its scheme would have been better received in another day. Even George admitted that his music had an "acid touch" which he felt gave added point to the lyrics, "in keeping with the satire of the piece."

But the public that had so admired the revised *Strike Up the Band* (191 performances) and *Of Thee I Sing* (441 performances), neither understood nor supported *Let 'Em Eat Cake* (90 performances). There were objections to everything, from the title to the scene in which Throttlebottom is almost guillotined. Many found George's music too intellectual, too contrapuntal, too much the servant of the book. There were no hit songs, they complained, although "Mine" became quite popular.

Only Ira Gershwin came off uniformly well in the reviews, for his work was readily recognized for its skill and deftness as well as the good-natured handling of the show's rather bitter ideas. His kindly sense of humor could not help making it all seem to be just a lot of fun.

The three political operettas marked a great advance in the development of the American musical, and it was no accident that these advances should have been made by the Gershwins. Even *Let 'Em Eat Cake,* though not appreciated, may one day be recognized for its excellence, both musical and lyrical. In it lie buried some of the best Gershwin ideas; in fact, many of the devices used by George for the first time in the political operettas were used again later by other composers with great success. But when they got around to using some of George's so-called "intellectual" musical ideas, the musical theatre had advanced to a point where such original ideas were taken for granted. Nor did they confuse people. In George's contrapuntal songs—such as "Mine," for example—there are two songs being sung at the same time: the ballad itself, and the countermelody, commenting upon the ballad. (Many years later Tommy Dorsey used this same idea in a recording of Irving Berlin's "Marie," which became a best-selling record.)

George and Ira Gershwin pioneered in the form that ten and twenty years later flowered into the great musicals of Rodgers and Hammerstein and the other long-run musicals that followed. The form of the political operettas were in their way the first American operas using American settings and characters, as well as the American language in the lyrics and American music holding it all together.

As for "American opera," George had been thinking about that for a long time. Having gained the experience on the political operettas, maybe, he felt, it was time for that "Gershwin opera" that everyone had been talking about for so long.

Chapter 13

"... I AM THINKING ABOUT WRITING AN OPERA ..."

Almost the instant he had become one of America's best-known composers George and the "American opera" were linked in everyone's mind. He was practically haunted by it. As early as 1923 he was interviewed by reporters as far off as London for his opinion on the possibility of "ragtime" opera and when it would come about. And if so, would George be the man for the job?

George had already made a step in that direction with *Blue Monday* of the year before, but he regarded that as a half step in the right direction; "laboratory work in American music," he called it.

Once jazz captured the American imagination in

the Twenties, and American artists and composers, as well as native themes, were taken seriously by critics, it seemed that someone was always announcing the future production of an American jazz opera. But the future never seemed to come. Otto Kahn, wealthy patron of the arts and a good friend of George's, hinted regularly for George to write a jazz opera for the Metropolitan Opera House (no less!). In fact, for a few exciting days in October 1929, it almost happened. George and the Metropolitan had practically signed the contracts for such a work, but it was learned that the work George had wanted to set to music was not available at the time. Curiously, it would hardly have resulted in a "jazz opera," for George had decided upon *The Dybbuk,* based upon a Jewish folk tale. He had composed some very interesting music for this opera, but never had the chance to use it in the Metropolitan Opera House. Instead he simply used some of the song ideas in musicals.

He was drawn, as he had been in *Blue Monday,* toward a story about the Negro. Composers before him in attempting to do the American opera made the mistake of trying to be about as American as they could get by writing about the Indian. The results were never happy.

For a time George had considered Eugene O'Neill's *The Emperor Jones* (which eventually was made into an opera by another composer); he also discussed a story possibility with Carl Van Vechten about Harlem, but that hadn't worked out either. Actually George had already made up his mind. He knew the story that he really wanted to make into an American opera.

That went back to 1926. He had come home one evening after a long day's rehearsal of *Oh, Kay!*; George was tired and he was tense. Rather than go out he settled down for an evening of reading, something he rarely did. He chose a small book, the best-selling first novel of a Southern poet, DuBose Heyward. The book was titled *Porgy*.

Something about the story captured George right away. He didn't stop reading until he completed the book, after which—it was now four in the morning—he was at his desk writing Heyward about how much he liked the book and suggesting that they collaborate on making an opera of *Porgy*.

Heyward, in North Carolina, was flattered to receive so warm a letter from the famed George Gershwin, particularly with the offer to set it to music. But someone else had already found dramatic material in the book. When he announced to his wife, Dorothy, that George Gershwin was interested in setting *Porgy* to music, Heyward learned that she had been secretly making a play of it. Unable to disappoint Dorothy, Hayward wrote to George, explaining what had happened.

George was not bothered; it would help if *Porgy* were a play, and besides, before he would tackle the kind of job he had in mind for *Porgy*, he wanted to study a good deal more. The last especially impressed Heyward, for in 1926 George had achieved, in Heyward's words, "a success that might have dazzled any man. . . ."

When the play was produced it proved to be a great success, but in the meantime George had become very busy with his several projects. The depression had come and most of the money Heyward had earned was wiped out in bank failures. A daughter had been born to the Heywards, so that he had an added responsibility.

Then one day, practically out of nowhere, came a letter from George. Dated March 29, 1932, it contained news that delighted Heyward. ". . . In thinking of ideas for new compositions, I came back to one that I had several years ago—namely, *Porgy*—and the thought of setting it to music."

Heyward replied, "I want to tell you again how pleased I am that you have returned to your original idea of doing a musical setting of *Porgy*.

"I would be tremendously interested in working on the book with you. . . . As to the lyrics, I am not so sure until I know more definitely what you have in mind. Perhaps your brother Ira would want to do them. Or maybe we could do them together. . . ."

Heyward was eager to begin, not only because of his bad financial state, but also the idea of working on a musical *Porgy* was an exciting challenge. But he was in for a slight jolt. When George wrote again it was to tell Heyward that he was happy also that the operatic rights to *Porgy* were clear, but that he could not actually begin work on it until January 1933—almost a year away.

George had already committed himself to do a score for Aarons and Freedley, there were concert appearances to make, and he had even signed a contract to appear on his own radio show, "Music by Gershwin."

The year actually dragged out to two. In that period George not only studied but he also did the show for Aarons and Freedley. Titled *Pardon My English,* it proved to be a disaster for the producers. It was so bad that the partnership broke up after ten successful years. Freedley even left the country. The problem with *Pardon My English* was the book. The Gershwins, in their usual innocence, did their very best but even that did not save the show.

George had been neglecting his concert composition so, for an All-Gershwin Concert at Lewisohn Stadium in the summer of 1932, he composed a short travel piece, the result of a trip to Havana, titled *Rumba.* While he was in Havana George had been fascinated by the Cuban percussion instruments which were then completely unknown in New York. When he returned to work on *Rumba* he brought with him samples of Cuban sticks, bongos, gourds and maracas. He composed *Rumba* during July, began the orchestration on the first of August and had the entire work ready for the Gershwin Concert on August 16.

In the meantime the ever-patient Heyward had taken a job in Hollywood writing movie scripts, for it was clear that George was not yet ready to begin work on *Porgy.*

George had his own jolt during this same period. Heyward learned that Al Jolson, the vaudeville star, was interested in playing in a musical version of *Porgy,* with himself cast as the crippled Negro. If this was to happen it would mean a great deal of money for Heyward. But before he even considered releasing *Porgy* to Jolson, Heyward wrote to George saying that if George could only begin soon, he would not let Jolson have the work.

George, however, felt that the musical that Jolson would have in mind would in no way interfere with the operatic production George wanted to do; therefore, "if you can see your way to making some ready money from Jolson's version" he suggested that Heyward give Jolson the rights.

George's understanding and reasonableness touched Heyward. "Please let me tell you," he wrote, "that I think your attitude in this matter is simply splendid. It makes me all the more eager to work with you some day, some time. . . ."

But it was not yet to be. There was another musical to do, this time *Let 'Em Eat Cake.* However, on October 26, 1933, contracts were signed with the Theatre Guild to produce the musical *Porgy.* On November 3rd, the Theatre Guild officially announced that George and Heyward were to collaborate on a musical *Porgy.*

The Jolson project had simply fallen through. Had

it not, it might have proved interesting, for Jolson had interested Jerome Kern and Oscar Hammerstein II in doing the songs. For Heyward it was just another in a series of disappointments.

At last, here was an actual contract! Now he was certain that *Porgy* would be set to music. A week after the papers had printed the announcement, Heyward had completed the first scene and sent it to George. George was busy rehearsing with the Pittsburgh Symphony Orchestra at the time and didn't even have time to write Heyward. When he did, on November 25, 1933, he confessed that he hadn't yet actually started composing any of the music.

He had already contracted for a cross-country tour with the Leo Reisman orchestra, a 12,000-mile junket that would begin in Boston on January 14, 1934, and would end in Brooklyn on February 26. For the tour he had decided to work up a special piece for himself, the *"I Got Rhythm" Variations* which he dedicated to Ira. In the main it proved to be a most successful tour, but a wearing one. George had a fine time playing the new *Variations,* one of his most ingenious compositions. But he was very tired when he returned to New York in February. He had nothing to look forward to but his weekly radio broadcast; he couldn't even get away to spend some time with DuBose.

On his piano were the pages of completed libretto that Heyward had so faithfully mailed him. George decided then and there: no more thinking about writing an opera, he would go to work.

Chapter 14

PORGY AND BESS

GEORGE began with good intentions, for he was heard to say that he planned to spend eight hours a day working on the opera. His busy life did not quite permit this, as it turned out. But once he went into action George concentrated all of his creative energies on *Porgy.*

When he finally was able to get down to the actual work in February 1934, all of the thinking he had done about the kind of opera *Porgy* should be made it possible for him to compose with a definite design in mind. Although he regarded *Porgy* as a kind of folk tale, George did not intend to use any actual folk songs in the score. He would compose every note himself. He did, however, want to visit Charleston to study the music there so that his music would honestly reflect the music of the people in Heyward's play. But he had not yet set any music on paper.

"I like to digest ideas a long time," he explained. "I am really only happy when I am composing or just finishing something."

On his way to a Florida vacation in December 1933, George stopped off in Charleston to see the Heywards. "I would like to see the town," he told DuBose, "and hear some spirituals and perhaps go to a colored café or two if there are any."

They went to a Negro church, and George was deeply impressed by the singing which was powerful in its simplicity. "It gave me a lot to think about," he commented after.

George was stretched in the sand on a Florida beach when a melody came to him literally out of the blue. It was the first of the *Porgy* music to come to him and, as it turned out, the first song in the opera, the lullaby "Summertime."

On his return trip to New York George again stopped with the Heywards. He and Heyward discussed the handling of the opera. George felt that all of it should be sung, Heyward did not agree. It was probably their only disagreement during the entire work, but George eventually won out. He left for home; it would be six months before George and DuBose would get together again.

In the meantime they collaborated by mail. Heyward would write the libretto based upon his and Dorothy's play. As soon as he completed a scene he would mail it to George for suggestions and—DuBose hoped—work. George's most frequent criticism was that he felt perhaps it was running too long. Heyward cut more and more of the play to make room for the music and the songs.

Because of the way they had to work, Heyward's original suggestion of having Ira help with the lyrics now proved to be very valuable. He edited Heyward's lyrics to help the poetry become song lyrics, for a poem is not necessarily a song. Heyward greatly respected Ira so there was no disagreement over this. In fact the collaboration of the Gershwins with DuBose Heyward was an unusual one and not the battle of egos that most collaborations become. There was nothing but mutual respect and close working together. George, however, dominated the entire project.

Heyward refused to leave Charleston, explaining that a new place, and particularly a place like New York, bothered him and interfered with his creative processes. George was forced to stay close to Rockefeller Center's Radio City rehearsing and appearing on his weekly broadcast. Otherwise, New York didn't bother him. He once said, however, that "the ideal room for composing would be one with four bare walls and no windows." Someone pointed out that his luxurious studio hardly filled that bill, especially with its panoramic view of New York. George replied, "The buildings are fixed and still. They don't disturb you."

That George could not get down to Charleston to study the local material firsthand troubled Heyward a little. "I am naturally disappointed," he wrote George, "that you have tied yourself up so long in New York.

I believe that if you had gotten down for a reasonably long stay and gotten deep into the sources here you would have done a bigger job. . . ."

In June 1934, George was free of his radio program for two months. Almost immediately after, he left with his cousin, the artist Henry Botkin, for Charleston. They deserted the conveniences of New York for the primitive living conditions of Folly Beach on an island just off Charleston. The Heywards had a summer home there; George and Harry rented a small four-room cottage nearby.

For five weeks George worked in that cottage while Harry painted. They were practically cut off from civilization. Even their water had to be brought in from Charleston. George worked in his room on a small upright piano that had also been transported from the mainland.

Although George more or less adapted himself to the primitive life—one paper called him the "bearded Folly Beach wild man"—he was primarily still the big-city boy. Unlike the skyscrapers of New York, the vistas of Folly Beach rarely remained "fixed and still." The ocean pounded the beach, the winds battered the palm trees (in later years it blew away the cottage in which Gershwin and Botkin had lived), the alligators roared in the swamps and the buzz of insects kept him awake at night.

Despite all this, George and Heyward progressed with the opera. They continued to make trips to nearby Negro churches. In Hendersonville, just as they were about to enter one, George stopped Heyward and whispered, "Listen!"

Inside, the choir was raising its assorted voices in a hymn; to Heyward it seemed to be a jumble. He had heard it many times before. George's keen ear had discovered that the choir was actually singing six different prayers at the same time in an amazing counterpoint. It was a remarkable effect that Heyward had taken for granted until George pointed it out to him. George made a note to use that same effect in the opera.

At another church at neighboring James Island George was so carried away by the singing that he joined in the "shouting," a very complex style of singing which combined not only the sound of the voice, but also the rhythmic stamping of the feet and clapping of the hands. The congregation enjoyed George's performance very much, especially since he proved to be a more expert shouter than their own expert.

When George and Harry returned to New York late in July, George was well along with the composing and had even begun a little of the orchestration. On January 30, 1935, George was able to announce, "The composition of *Porgy* is finished and I intend to work on the orchestrations at Palm Beach." He later reported from Florida in a letter to Ira that the work came "slowly, there being millions of notes to write."

Excitement was beginning to mount, for the time was drawing near for cast auditions, as well as all the other details that went into the production of an opera.

Sets would have to be designed, a director appointed, theatres booked, and a rehearsal period set. In April, DuBose Heyward came north to assist with the casting, for not only did its members have to be able to sing, they must look like the characters Heyward had invented. For Porgy they chose a music teacher from Washington, D. C., the baritone Todd Duncan; Bess was a student of singing, Anne Brown; the villain Crown a former concert singer from Boston, Warren Coleman. The only important role not filled by a trained musician was that of Sportin' Life, which was given to John W. Bubbles of the vaudeville team of Buck and Bubbles. Rehearsals were due to begin in August.

To George the spring and summer months of 1935 were a blur of activity: there were "millions of notes," indeed. Luckily he was able to depend upon help from Kay Swift, who unselfishly set aside her own work to give George a hand with copying, checking, editing and just about any other chore that would relieve him of the drudgery and give him time to concentrate on the orchestrations. Also an excellent pianist, she was able to join George in testing the sound of certain passages by playing them on the pianos in his studio.

George's old friend Dr. Albert Sirmay also pitched in to lend a hand in preparing the music for publication. There was much painstaking proofreading to be done and copies of the music to be sent to the singers and the conductor, Alexander Smallens. They were all racing against time.

George, especially, was aware of the time. As he completed a scene's orchestration he carefully dated it, as if he was also aware of the opera's historical importance. Finally at the end of the bulky yet neat manuscript George wrote: "Finished August 23, 1935."

Rehearsals were already under way. The problem of the title came up. It was possible that some people might think the opera was merely a revival of the original play; they would be confused. Ira solved the problem by suggesting *Porgy and Bess,* to which George brightly agreed, commenting that it was right in the operatic tradition. There had been, after all, *Orfeo ed Euridice, Tristan und Isolde, Pelleas et Melisande;* why not *Porgy and Bess?*

There it was—over 500 pages of George Gershwin's *Porgy and Bess,* after the years of talk, plans and work, ready to be sung.

On September 30, 1935, four days after his thirty-seventh birthday, George watched the world premiere performance at the Colonial Theater in Boston. Two years of hard, and inspired, work had gone into those three hours of music. In fact, the hard work had continued practically up to the moment of curtain time.

Porgy and Bess ran too long in the rehearsals, close to four hours. There would have to be cuts. George defended his work, but he knew he had to permit the cuts that Mamoulian was suggesting. (Rouben Mamoulian was the director who had also staged the original *Porgy.*) He knew that some of the best musical passages would have to go, but they had to shorten the running time of the opera.

Out went the original opening piano music, out went "The Buzzard Song," out went the six-voiced prayer, out went the trio "Oh, Where's My Bess?" although Porgy's solo version remained. There were several other slashings that finally put *Porgy and Bess* into what was considered to be better running shape.

George gave in reluctantly, though without any display of temperament, whatever his feelings about the songs and the work that only he knew had gone into them.

The opening night audience in Boston greeted *Porgy and Bess* with great enthusiasm. Serge Koussevitzky, the distinguished conductor of the Boston Symphony, hailed it as "a great advance in American opera." One newspaper critic expressed the opinion that "Gershwin must now be accepted as a serious composer," while another found *Porgy and Bess* to be his "most important contribution to music."

The New York critics did not agree.

The newspapers, recognizing the importance of the event, sent both drama critics and music critics to the opening. There was no real agreement among them. *Porgy and Bess* simply did not fit into any neat little category; it seemed to be part opera and part musical comedy. Or maybe it was neither. Whatever it was, most critics didn't like it. Some composers, particularly, envious of George's popular music successes, found just about everything wrong with it.

This kind of reception was not good for the box office. *Porgy and Bess* ran for 124 performances at the
Alvin Theatre, once the home of so many Gershwin
hits. It then was sent on a short tour and closed in
Washington, D. C., on March 21, 1936. *Porgy and Bess*
lost $70,000. George did not earn enough money from
it to pay for the costs of having the orchestrations
copied.

This was a bitter disappointment. He knew that he
had put his very best into the opera. He took some
consolation from the fact that the 124 performances
were a great deal more than it might have had at the
Metropolitan Opera House. Also, the full score was
published by his own Gershwin Publishing Corpora-
tion. At least all those hard-won millions of notes were
safely on paper. Someday someone would rediscover
Porgy and Bess.

Worn out and emotionally exhausted from all the
work and the trials of rehearsals and opening nights,
George went off to Mexico for a few weeks to get some
sun and perhaps get some ideas for a new work. He returned to New York in the middle of December, not
very enthused by the Indian music he had heard in
Mexico. The *Porgy* cast met him at the docks with
Gershwin song; he was enthused about that.

George, as was usual with him, went to the next
project. He was signed to appear as piano soloist with
the Philadelphia Symphony on January 21st, while
Porgy and Bess would also be in Philadelphia. For the
occasion George put together a "Suite from Porgy and

Bess," in five sections. Alexander Smallens, conductor of the opera, conducted the first performance of the suite (which has since been renamed by Ira Gershwin *Catfish Row,* George's title for the first section). George performed as piano soloist in the *Concerto.* Unfortunately the concert was not very well attended and the new piece was scarcely noticed. Later, however, when George introduced the suite to Washington (February 9, 1936) the hall was crowded and he was cheered so enthusiastically that he was happy to make a mock complaint, "I have bowed so much that my back feels broken."

George went on to repeat the same sensation with the suite at St. Louis, Boston, Chicago, San Francisco and Detroit. People left the concerts singing strains of *Porgy and Bess.* George was proving to be his own best propagandist. People only needed a little time and the opportunity to hear the music. He was pleased to hear the songs on the radio.

By the spring of 1936 George and Ira were becoming a little restless. Ira did have a hit running on Broadway, the *Ziegfeld Follies of 1936,* with music by their friend Vernon Duke; the hit song from the show was "I Can't Get Started." But that, like *Porgy and Bess,* was the past. The Gershwins were thinking of new things to do. For a while they discussed the idea of writing a screenplay and the songs for a film musical. They hadn't been to Hollywood since their unhappy experience with *Delicious* in 1931.

The movies had come a long way since then. In just

five short years the moviemakers had learned how to make very charming film musicals using better-than-average songs. After his sister had retired from show business, Fred Astaire had drifted about a little and then almost accidentally formed a dancing partnership with Ginger Rogers. Their musicals were now the rage of Hollywood, and very popular with the public. Their songs were written only by the finest of song-writers—Vincent Youmans, Jerome Kern and Irving Berlin.

The Gershwins would consider doing another film musical, if they could find such fresh material as those offered by the Astaire-Rogers films. The offer naturally came and, once the contracts were agreed upon, the Gershwins made plans to leave as soon as George fulfilled his obligation to appear at Lewisohn Stadium in the Gershwin Concert, which had now become an annual event.

On August 10, 1936, George and Ira boarded a plane in Newark for Hollywood, land of the happy endings.

Chapter 15

HOLLYWOOD

Gⴠᴇᴏʀɢᴇ was not happy in Hollywood. To begin with, he had come there knowing that he was
regarded as a "highbrow" composer, perhaps too highbrow for the kind of musicals Hollywood was turning
out.

Nor could George find enough to keep him very
busy in the lax and easy atmosphere of the film capital.
As soon as they arrived, George and Ira went to work
on songs for the Astaire-Rogers movie, then titled *Step-
ping Toes*. A month later, after they had settled in a
fine house at 1019 Roxbury Drive, they were still waiting for a script of the film.

To George this seemed a peculiar way to work, ac-
customed as he was to working from the books of
Broadway musicals, no matter how slender the plot.
The slow pace, however, suited Ira perfectly. Naturally

easygoing, he found the climate and the pace very nice indeed. They had arrived in August 1936; in November they were writing the final song for the picture. At this point it no longer had a title. Another future plan was for a ballet George would compose.

It never came about, but their friend Vincente Minnelli suggested *Shall We Dance?* as a title which everyone liked. George's long Latin-American composition, which was to have been the ballet, was discarded by the studio. But George managed to write a brief instrumental piece, "Walking the Dog," in which he satirized the Hollywood practice of using giant orchestras for background music. George scored the piece for a chamber orchestra of less than a dozen instruments.

It was December before he was able to say that the "Astaire picture is practically finished and so far everybody is happy." He then referred to a sore spot, "The studio, realizing Gershwin can be lowbrow, has just taken up their option on our contract for the next Astaire movie. . . ."

There were other offers, too. George and Ira decided to do the next Astaire musical and were also planning for another, to be produced by Samuel Goldwyn.

They had begun *A Damsel in Distress,* the next Astaire film for RKO Radio Pictures, when George saw the finished *Shall We Dance?* George was disappointed and complained, "The picture does not take advantage of the songs as well as it could."

In May, 1937, they finished eight songs for *A Damsel in Distress* and almost immediately started work on what George called "a super, super, stupendous moving picture extravaganza," *The Goldwyn Follies*. He was joking, though, hoping that the Gershwin songs and music might be given better treatment than they received in the first two movies.

The steady assignments the Gershwins were getting should have kept them constantly busy, but this did not prove to be true. Unlike work on a show, where the songwriters are constantly consulted, the Gershwins' work on a movie was considered finished as soon as the songs were turned in. They always seemed to keep ahead of the scriptwriters and, when George offered suggestions that might have contributed to the film, the studio ears were deaf.

He missed the excitement of New York. When he wasn't working with Ira he was taking hikes with his dog Tony, or he joined the groups around the Gershwin swimming pool or at parties. George was happy that so many of his New York friends were in Hollywood, which made up a little for his boredom. His boyhood heroes, Irving Berlin and Jerome Kern, were there and George reported that he saw a great deal of them. He made several photographs of Irving Berlin and himself. He was also at work on an oil painting of Jerome Kern and another of a new friend, the great modern composer Arnold Schönberg.

Oscar Levant was in Hollywood too, to study with Schönberg and to compose a movie score. They had been good friends in New York where Levant and

George tested many a new Gershwin composition at the two pianos in Gershwin's apartment.

Another friend was composer Harold Arlen, whose "Stormy Weather" was one of George's favorite songs. They admired each other's work and became even warmer friends than they had been in New York. George was planning to paint a portrait of Arlen's lovely wife, Anya, but just never got to it.

Seeing the Arlens, as well as Lee and Ira, only reminded George of his own loneliness. He discussed marriage with Arlen, who advised George not to marry because of George's overriding interest in himself and his work. George rejected this advice rather angrily and seriously began searching for a possible Mrs. Gershwin.

He formed fleeting friendships with starlets, among them the enchanting French actress Simone Simon, but little came of these. He had what amounted to a schoolboy crush on Paulette Goddard, who was then married to comedian Charlie Chaplin and not terribly interested in divorcing a member of Hollywood's royalty for a composer.

The values of Hollywood caused George much pain. In New York, in London, and Paris, he was George Gershwin, one of America's important composers, a worldwide celebrity. In Hollywood, he was just another songwriter turning out songs for the real celebrities, the stars.

George tried to keep himself busy with other work. Not only did he make several concert appearances all over the country, he also began making plans for other concerts well into 1938 that would take him to Europe. He also began talking about, and even sketching themes, for new concert pieces—he wanted to do a symphony, a ballet, a string quartet. He even suggested to DuBose Heyward that he come up with another libretto for an opera. There were plans for a future Broadway show also.

The failure of *Porgy and Bess* continued to haunt him. He was saddened to learn that a European tour of the opera could not take place. "I have a feeling," he quietly said, "that it might prove to be a sensation all through Europe." He was never to know how right he was.

On January 9, 1937, he wrote to Emily Paley in New York. He told her how much he missed her and Lou and hoped they would come out to visit. He was in a more typical Gershwin mood when he reported that an All-Gershwin Concert was being planned for "Feb. 10 & 11th. We shall have Todd Duncan come out for these & sing some of 'Porgy' music. I wish you could come. Not to sing—just to be here."

George hoped that the concert in Los Angeles would stir up some movie interest in *Porgy and Bess*. It was an interesting concert; Alexander Smallens conducted the *Cuban Overture* and *An American in Paris;* George appeared as piano soloist in the *Rhapsody in Blue* and the *Concerto in F*. It was while he was playing the concerto that something unusual happened.

Oscar Levant was one of the few people who were

aware of what had happened. "Though George had played the 'Concerto' dozens of times in public with great fluency," Levant later recalled, "I noticed that he stumbled on a very easy passage in the first movement. Then, in the andante, in playing the four simple octaves that conclude the movement above the sustained orchestral chords, he blundered again." This was extremely unusual for George, who was always practically note perfect in his playing. The only explanation he offered to Levant after the concert was a joking remark that he had been thinking of Levant at the time which was enough to throw him off.

George was complaining a lot by then. But people had long ago become used to his concern for his health. They suffered along with him with his composer's stomach and his addiction to strange health foods. He began to worry about his hair. He was only thirty-eight and much too young to be losing his hair. He bought a strange machine into which he placed his head for massage.

But worst of all he was not himself, he was irritable, at times short-tempered and complaining. Lee Gershwin then insisted that he take a physical checkup, which to everyone's relief, found him in good health. Obviously George's dissatisfaction with work in Hollywood was showing itself in this way. He complained of very severe headaches. One night after a party, Lee and Ira had stayed behind to say goodbye to the host as George walked out ahead of them. They found him sitting on the curb holding his head and complaining of a headache.

Then late in June, 1937, George and Ira visited the Goldwyn Studios to see how the picture was coming along. George collapsed while they were there. Again he was given a physical, a very thorough one—complete except for a spinal tap. George would not permit that, for he had heard it was painful. Some of his symptoms pointed toward a possible brain tumor and only a spinal tap could settle that question. Otherwise George was in excellent health.

Perhaps it was a mental problem. He was restless, lonely and unhappy. His headaches could easily come from that. He saw a psychiatrist, who strongly believed George's illness was a physical and not a mental one.

The headaches continued and some days his coordination was so bad that he couldn't play the piano. It was obvious that George was seriously ill. Ira got them released from the Goldwyn contract, hoping that George would improve after a rest. For all the boredom that George complained of, he still had been living at a grueling pace composing and moving about the country on his concert tours.

A few days of quiet and George seemed to improve. He moved out of the Gershwin house on Roxbury Drive into the home of lyricist and friend E. Y. Harburg, where George could get away from the excitement of the Gershwin house. Only Lee and Ira would visit him. There was talk about the new songs and the future.

It was early July, 1937. On Friday, July 9th, George fell into a coma and was rushed to the hospital. An emergency operation revealed the suspected tumor in the brain. But it had gone too far; on a wet, dark Sunday morning—July 11, 1937—the brilliant flame that had been the life of George Gershwin went out.

Chapter 16

CODA

GEORGE Gershwin once said, in a typically youthful remark, that he had more tunes in his head than could be written down in a lifetime. It was, at the time, an amusing—and true—comment but how was anyone to know that his lifetime would last a mere thirty-eight years?

When he died Gershwin left a rich legacy, although for a long time after, it could not compensate for the loss to Ira, to their mother, Frankie, Arthur, to Lee and to the many close friends who knew and loved him.

George's legacy is his music, in the songs that for some reason never have become dated as have so many others written at the same time. They have the quality of classics. There are hundreds of Gershwin's songs yet unknown that will one day be rediscovered. Over half a hundred remain unpublished, carefully watched by the publisher and Ira awaiting that right musical. It is as if the intensity of Gershwin's work has kept some part of him alive after 1937. If anything, his music is better known and even more popular than it was during his all too brief lifetime.

When he called himself "a modern romantic," George Gershwin summed up his place in music much better than all the learned words written about him by musicologists and critics. Gershwin's talent only seemed to confuse them, for they never could understand that it was a natural expression as normal as breathing and as simple and direct as a flower. There was little artificiality in Gershwin's music; this may have confused critics but it never confused those who love Gershwin's music.

Of the concert works, the *Rhapsody in Blue, Concerto in F* and *An American in Paris* have all become part of the standard repertoire of all the major symphony orchestras throughout the world. They are accepted as important contributions to American music.

It is one of Gershwin's achievements that he focused serious attention upon the American composer and his works. He helped to pave a path into the concert halls, a path that had been little traveled by the contemporary American composer before Gershwin came on the scene.

Gershwin's personality was fine public relations for both the American composer and his music. He was young, jaunty, had a sense of humor, did not wear his hair long, smoked cigars and pipes and wore blue shirts. He laughed a lot and could hold his own in a tennis match, golf game or a round of boxing. He was young, indeed, and he was handsome and wealthy, the typical American son of Russian immigrants. These were qualities that were greatly admired, especially during the Twenties.

George carried his success well. He could always judge his own work with an almost shocking detachment. If he liked something of his he said so, if not he also said so. It was not ego, but an understanding and appreciation of his own talents. He was not, however, so busy that he could not put in a good word with a publisher about the songs of another composer. And when he had his own radio show, he furnished many younger composers with an outlet for their work by presenting their songs to a wide audience. Among his guests were such composers as Harold Arlen and Morton Gould—as well as his own younger brother Arthur. George was also free with money, which he lent to young struggling songwriters.

One of the tragedies of his early death is that he never lived to witness the success that he himself had predicted for *Porgy and Bess*. Its several revivals would have pleased him, but the one produced by Robert Breen and Blevins Davis which triumphantly toured the United States, Canada, South America and Europe would have thrilled him. *Porgy and Bess* was acclaimed everywhere the company appeared, from Paris to the Middle East to Moscow. It was cheered in Milan at La

Scala. In this historic opera house, *Porgy and Bess*
made more history: it was the first American opera
ever to play there, it was the first opera ever to run for
a week (La Scala was founded in 1778), it was the first
opera ever applauded during the performance. One
Italian critic called *Porgy and Bess* one of "the master-
works of the lyric theatre." It is without doubt the
most universally known, best-loved musical work by
an American composer.

Even Hollywood rediscovered Gershwin. In 1946,
Ira Gershwin, with the help of Kay Swift, who probably knows more Gershwin songs than anyone (next to
Ira, of course) and who has saved many from oblivion,
chose a number of George's notebook melodies for the
movie score, *The Shocking Miss Pilgrim*. In 1950, a
beautiful movie musical, *An American in Paris*, using an
all-Gershwin score, was produced and went on to win the
Academy Award as the best picture of the year. In
1957, Fred Astaire starred in a filmed *Funny Face*
(same title, but not the same show as his hit of thirty
years before). Many of the original songs were used
and proved to be the finest in the score.

One of the songs from *An American in Paris*, "Love
Is Here to Stay" (originally written for *The Goldwyn
Follies*), became very popular in the Fifties. It was the
last song George Gershwin ever wrote. Twelve years
later it was as fresh and lovely as when he first composed it.

The vitality and honesty of his imagination will
know no ending. George Gershwin is his music. Any-

one who really wants to know him will find him in the strains of the *Rhapsody in Blue,* the *Concerto in F, An American in Paris,* the *Second Rhapsody,* the *"I Got Rhythm" Variations* and a hundred songs. They sing of a young, jaunty, romantic man, happy only when he was busy or finishing something. His music reflects his personality even better than his photographs.

Both, Gershwin's personality and his music, are being rediscovered by new generations that had never known the Jazz Age. Their feelings are best expressed by a member of George's own generation, the writer John O'Hara. Like Gershwin, O'Hara is sensitive and poetic, but he could never be sentimental. He said, "George Gershwin died on July 11, 1937, but I don't have to believe it if I don't want to."

THE WORKS OF GEORGE GERSHWIN

The following is a chronological listing of Gershwin's important works. This includes individual songs, scores for shows and concert works.

1916

"When You Want 'Em, You Can't Get 'Em, When You've Got 'Em, You Don't Want 'Em"—lyric by Murray Roth. (Gershwin's first published song.)

1917

Rialto Ripples, piano rag solo, written with Will Donaldson. (Gershwin's first published instrumental number.)

1918

"The Real American Folk Song (Is a Rag)"—lyric by Ira Gershwin. (The first all-Gershwin song to be heard in a show; introduced in *Ladies First.*)

Half Past Eight. (Gershwin's first musical; closed in Syracuse, N. Y.)

1919

"I Was So Young (You Were So Beautiful)"—lyric by Irving Caesar and Al Bryan. (The first Gershwin song to become popular; introduced in the musical comedy, *Good Morning, Judge.*)

La La Lucille, musical comedy with lyrics by Arthur Jackson and B. G. DeSylva. (Gershwin's first complete score and first musical comedy hit. The outstanding song: "Nobody But You.")

"Swanee"—lyric by Irving Caesar. (Gershwin's most successful song hit; first sung in *The Capitol Revue,* later interpolated by Al Jolson into *Sinbad.*)

1920

George White's Scandals, a revue with lyrics by Arthur Jackson. (The first in a series of five *Scandals* scores. Outstanding songs: "On My Mind the Whole Night Long," "The Songs of Long Ago" and "Scandal Walk.")

"Waiting For the Sun to Come Out"—lyric by Ira Gershwin. (The first published George and Ira Gershwin song; introduced in the musical, *The Sweetheart Shop.*)

1921

George White's Scandals, a revue with lyrics by Arthur Jackson. (Outstanding songs: "Drifting Along With the Tide" and "South Sea Isles.")

A Dangerous Maid, musical with lyrics by Arthur Francis (Ira Gershwin). (The first Gershwin collaboration on a show score; the musical closed in Pittsburgh. Outstanding songs: "The Simple Life" and "Boy Wanted.")

1922

"Do It Again"—lyric by B. G. DeSylva. (Introduced in the musical, *The French Doll.*)

George White's Scandals, revue with lyrics by B. G. DeSylva and E. Ray Goetz. (Outstanding songs: "I'll Build a Stairway to Paradise"—lyric by DeSylva and Ira Gershwin, and "Where Is the Man of My Dreams?" For this *Scandals* Gershwin composed the one-act opera, *Blue Monday,* later retitled *135th Street.*)

Our Nell, musical comedy with lyrics by Brian Hooker; music by Gershwin and William Daly. (Outstanding songs: "Innocent Ingenue Baby," "By and By," and "Walking Home With Angeline.")

1923

George White's Scandals, revue with lyrics by B. G. DeSylva, E. Ray Goetz and Ballard MacDonald. (Outstanding song: "Where Is She?")

1924

Sweet Little Devil, musical comedy with lyrics by B. G. DeSylva. (Outstanding song: "Virginia.")

Rhapsody in Blue, for piano and orchestra. (Orchestrated by Ferde Grofé.)

George White's Scandals, revue with lyrics by B. G. DeSylva and Ballard MacDonald. (Outstanding song: "Somebody Loves Me.")

Primrose, musical comedy with lyrics by Desmond Carter and Ira Gershwin. (Gershwin's first hit musical in London. Outstanding songs: "Isn't It Wonderful?," "Four Little Sirens" and "Wait a Bit, Susie.")

Lady, Be Good, musical comedy with lyrics by Ira Gershwin. (The first complete musical by the Gershwin brothers and a great success. Outstanding songs: "Fascinating Rhythm," "So Am I," "Oh, Lady Be Good!," "The Half of It, Dearie Blues" and "The Man I Love.")

1925

Short Story, for violin and piano. (Arranged by Samuel Dushkin.)

Tell Me More, musical comedy with lyrics by Ira Gershwin and B. G. DeSylva. (Outstanding songs: "Three Times a Day" and "Kickin' the Clouds Away.")

Concerto in F, for piano and orchestra.

Tip Toes, musical comedy with lyrics by Ira Gershwin. (Outstanding songs: "Looking For a Boy," "When Do We Dance?," "These Charming People," "That Certain Feeling" and "Sweet and Low-Down.")

Song of the Flame, musical comedy with lyrics by Oscar Hammerstein II and Otto Harbach; music by Gershwin and Herbert Stothart. (Outstanding songs: "Song of the Flame," "Cossack Love Song" and "Vodka.")

1926

"That Lost Barbershop Chord"—lyric by Ira Gershwin. (Introduced in the revue, *Americana.*)

Oh, Kay!, musical comedy with lyrics by Ira Gershwin. (Outstanding songs: "Dear Little Girl," "Maybe," "Clap Yo' Hands," "Do Do Do" and "Someone to Watch Over Me.")

Three Preludes, for piano.

1927

Strike Up the Band, political operetta with lyrics by Ira Gershwin. (The first version of this musical closed in Philadelphia. Outstanding song: "Seventeen and Twenty-one.")

Funny Face, musical comedy with lyrics by Ira Gershwin. (Outstanding songs: "High Hat," "Let's Kiss and Make Up," "Funny Face," " 'S Wonderful," "He Loves and She Loves" and "My One and Only.")

1928

Rosalie, musical comedy with lyrics by Ira Gershwin and P. G. Wodehouse; music by Gershwin and Sigmund Romberg. (Outstanding songs: "Say So!," "Oh Gee! Oh Joy!" and "How Long Has This Been Going On?")

Treasure Girl, musical comedy with lyrics by Ira Gershwin. (Outstanding songs: "I've Got a Crush on You," "Oh, So Nice," "I Don't Think I'll Fall in Love Today" and "Where's the Boy? Here's the Girl!")

An American in Paris, tone poem for orchestra.

1929

Show Girl, musical comedy with lyrics by Ira Gershwin and Gus Kahn. (Outstanding songs: "Do What You Do!" and "Liza.")

"In the Mandarin's Orchid Garden"—lyric by Ira Gershwin.

1930

Strike Up the Band, political operetta with lyrics by Ira Gershwin. (Revised version of the 1927 show. Outstanding songs: "Soon," "Strike Up the Band" and "I Want to Be a War Bride.")

Girl Crazy, musical comedy with lyrics by Ira Gershwin. (Outstanding songs: "Bidin' My Time," "Could You Use Me?" "Embraceable You," "Sam and Delilah," "I Got Rhythm," "But Not For Me," "Treat Me Rough" and "Boy! What Love Has Done to Me!")

1931

Delicious, film musical with lyrics by Ira Gershwin. (Outstanding songs: "Blah Blah Blah" and "Somebody From Somewhere.")

Of Thee I Sing, political operetta with lyrics by Ira Gershwin. (First musical to be given the Pulitzer Prize. Outstanding songs: "Wintergreen For President," "Because, Because," "Love Is Sweeping the Country," "Of Thee I Sing, Baby" and "Who Cares?")

Second Rhapsody, for orchestra with piano.

1932

Cuban Overture, for orchestra. (Original title: *Rumba.*)

Piano Transcriptions of 18 Songs, for solo piano. (Published as *George Gershwin's Song Book*: Simon and Schuster.)

1933

Pardon My English, musical comedy with lyrics by Ira Gershwin. (Outstanding songs: "Lorelei," "Isn't It a Pity?," "My Cousin in Milwaukee" and "So What?")

Let 'Em Eat Cake, political operetta with lyrics by Ira Gershwin. (Outstanding songs: "Mine," "Blue, Blue, Blue" and "Union Square.")

1934

"I Got Rhythm" Variations, for piano and orchestra.

1935

Porgy and Bess, opera with lyrics by DuBose Heyward and Ira Gershwin. (Outstanding songs: "Summertime," "A Woman Is a Sometime Thing," "My Man's Gone Now," "I Got Plenty o' Nothin'," "Bess, You Is My Woman Now," "It Ain't Necessarily So," "I Loves You, Porgy," "There's a Boat Dat's Leavin' Soon For New York," "Oh, Where's My Bess?" and "I'm On My Way.")

1936

Catfish Row, suite for orchestra. (Gershwin's own suite from *Porgy and Bess.*)

"By Strauss"—lyrics by Ira Gershwin. (Introduced in the revue, *The Show Is On.*)

Shall We Dance?, film musical with lyrics by Ira Gershwin. (Outstanding songs: "Let's Call the Whole Thing Off," "Shall We Dance?," "Slap That Bass," "They All Laughed," "Beginner's Luck" and "They Can't Take That Away From Me.")

1937

A Damsel in Distress, film musical with lyrics by Ira Gershwin. (Outstanding songs: "A Foggy Day," "I Can't Be Bothered Now," "The Jolly Tar and the

Milk Maid," "Nice Work If You Can Get It," "Stiff Upper Lip" and "Things Are Looking up.")

The Goldwyn Follies, film musical with lyrics by Ira Gershwin; additional music by Vernon Duke. (Outstanding songs: "I Love to Rhyme," "I Was Doing All Right," "Just Another Rhumba," "Love Is Here to Stay" and "Love Walked In.")

1946

The Shocking Miss Pilgrim, film musical with lyrics by Ira Gershwin. (Score consisted of unpublished Gershwin songs edited by Kay Swift. Outstanding songs: "Aren't You Kind of Glad We Did?," "The Back Bay Polka," "Changing My Tune," "For You, For Me, For Evermore" and "One, Two, Three.")

SELECTED GERSHWIN DISCOGRAPHY

All of Gershwin's concert works have been recorded, many in several versions of varying quality. The following discography is not intended to be a complete listing of the recordings of Gershwin's works which, including the songs, would run into the hundreds. Instead the discography lists the few outstanding recordings of each work (in the author's opinion), either for reasons of excellence of interpretation or history. The recordings are listed in order of preference.

Concert Works

Rhapsody in Blue (1924)

—George Gershwin, piano solo (piano roll): 20th Fox 3013 (Reverse: Songs, *Strike Up the Band* Rehearsal).

—George Gershwin, pianist: Distinguished Recordings 107 (also contains Kickin' the Clouds Away, That Certain Feeling, Sweet and Low-Down, and four popular songs by other composers).

—Reid Nibley, pianist, Maurice Abravanel conducting the Utah Symphony: Westminster 18687 (Reverse: *An American in Paris*).

—Eugene List, pianist, Howard Hanson conducting the Rochester Symphony: Mercury 50138 (Reverse: *Concerto in F*).

—Oscar Levant, pianist, Eugene Ormandy conducting the Philadelphia Symphony: Columbia CL-700 (Also: *An American in Paris;* Reverse: *Concerto in F*).

The solo piano version of this work by Gershwin himself is an astonishing re-creation from piano rolls; it is surprisingly lifelike and betrays little of the mechanical piano. This recording belongs in all Gershwin record collections. The playing by Reid Nibley captures some of Gershwin's poetic yet crisp playing style and the Westminster is very hi-fi. Eugene List does not quite have the Gershwin touch, but he is a fine pianist and is well supported by Hanson and the orchestra. Oscar Levant's performances are now a couple of decades old so that the recording may sound antiquated, but the recording is important because of Levant's long association with the works—and it is a bargain, containing as it does the three major Gershwin concert works.

Concerto in F (1925)

—Earl Wild, pianist, with Arthur Fiedler conducting the Boston Pops Orchestra: RCA Victor LM-2586 (also contains *"I Got Rhythm" Variations* and *Cuban Overture*).

—Reid Nibley, pianist, Maurice Abravanel conducting the Utah Symphony: Westminster 18685 (Reverse: *Rhapsody in Blue*).

—Eugene List, pianist, Howard Hanson conducting the Rochester Symphony: Mercury 50138 (Reverse: *Rhapsody in Blue*).

—Oscar Levant, pianist, André Kostelanetz conducting the New York Philharmonic: Columbia CL-700 (With *Rhapsody in Blue* and *An American in Paris*).

The Wild-Fiedler-Boston Pops interpretation is the finest available recording of the *Concerto;* technically the recording itself is remarkable. Wild's piano playing is exactly right for the work. The orchestration of the concerto, which was Gershwin's first attempt in a larger work, comes out clearly in the Westminster recording. While the pacing of the work may seem rather slow under Abravanel's direction, the interpretation is very poetic and certainly presents Gershwin's work in an interesting light. The List-Hanson version is a worthy interpretation, though List's playing at times is a little glib. The Levant-Kostelanetz recording is an interesting collaboration by two friends of Gershwin; the recording is no longer the highest of fi.

Preludes for Piano (1926)

—Leo Smit, pianist: Dot 3111 (coupled with other

jazz-inspired compositions by Stravinsky, Copland, Hindemith, Milhaud and Tansman).

This very interesting collection is somewhat mistitled "The Masters Write Jazz," and contains many pieces written around the same period when Gershwin was also composing in the jazz vein. Leo Smit is a fine young American pianist with the right approach to these pieces.

An American in Paris

—Arthur Fiedler conducting the Boston Pops: RCA Victor LM-2367 (Reverse: *Rhapsody in Blue*).

—Maurice Abravanel conducting the Utah Symphony: Westminster 18687 (Reverse: *Rhapsody in Blue*).

—Arturo Toscanini conducting the NBC Symphony: RCA-Victor LM-9020 (Reverse: Prokofiev's *Classical Symphony*).

The Fiedler-Boston Pops is full of the right zest and is excellently recorded. The Abravanel-Utah exhibits much the same quality although the group is not as expert as the Pops. The Toscanini-NBC is listed because it is an interesting performance, the only one of a Gershwin work by the great conductor. All of these show off Gershwin's skill as an orchestrator to great advantage.

Second Rhapsody (1931)

—Leonard Pennario, pianist, with Alfred Newman

conducting the Hollywood Bowl Symphony Or-
chestra: Capitol P-8581 (also contains *"I Got
Rhythm" Variations,* and arrangements by Greig
McRichie for piano and orchestra of themes from
Porgy and Bess and the *Cuban Overture*).

—Sondra Bianca, pianist, Hans-Jurgen Walther con-
ducting the Pro-Musica Symphony: M-G-M 3307
(Also: *Preludes, Cuban Overture* and *"I Got
Rhythm" Variations*).

The superb, excellently recorded *Second Rhapsody*
with Leonard Pennario at the piano is not only readily
available, but by far the finest produced to date. Unfortunately the Sondra Bianca recording of the *Second Rhapsody* has been deleted from M-G-M's catalog.
It is listed because copies may yet be found in some
record shops. It is a good performance, though not a
great one, and the recording itself is technically none
too good. An even better recording by Oscar Levant
and Morton Gould was once available on a ten-inch
Columbia Record.

Cuban Overture (1932)

—Arthur Fiedler conducting the Boston Pops Orchestra: RCA Victor LM-2586 (also contains *Concerto
in F* and *"I Got Rhythm" Variations*).

—Howard Hanson conducting the Rochester Sym-
phony: Mercury MG-50166 (Also: Gould's *Latin-
American Symphonette* and McBride's *Mexican
Rhapsody*).

—Louis Lane conducting the Cleveland Pops: Epic 3626 (Reverse: Latin American works by Gould, Bernstein, Lecuona, Villa-Lobos, etc.).

With the release of the Fiedler-Pops version of this work we finally have the definitive recording of it. Excellent recording techniques bring out the right balance of textures without obscuring the percussion instruments that Gershwin wanted to feature. Both of the other recordings are very good, both musically and technically. The Lane-Cleveland Pops recording brings a more interesting group of works, although most are mere snippets.

Piano Transcriptions of 18 Songs (1932)
  —Leonid Hambro, pianist: Walden 200.

This collection consists of Gershwin's special arrangements of the following songs: "Swanee," "Nobody But You," "I'll Build a Stairway to Paradise," "Do It Again," "Fascinating Rhythm," "Oh, Lady Be Good!," "Somebody Loves Me," "Sweet and Low-Down," "That Certain Feeling," "The Man I Love," "Clap Yo' Hands," "Do Do Do," "My One and Only," " 'S Wonderful," "Strike Up the Band," "Liza," "I Got Rhythm" and "Who Cares?" Concert pianist Leonid Hambro performs these miniatures in an affectionate recreation of Gershwin's playing style. The recording is a good reproduction of piano tone.

"I Got Rhythm" Variations (1934)
  —Earl Wild, pianist, with Arthur Fiedler conducting

the Boston Pops Orchestra: RCA Victor LM-2586 (also contains *Concerto in F* and *Cuban Overture*).

—Leonard Pennario, pianist, with Alfred Newman conducting the Hollywood Bowl Symphony Orchestra: Capitol P-8581 (also contains *Second Rhapsody* and arrangements of *Porgy and Bess* themes and the *Cuban Overture* for piano and orchestra).

—Buddy Weed, pianist, Paul Whiteman conducting his orchestra: Coral 57021 (Also: *Rhapsody in Blue* and *Cuban Overture*).

—Sondra Bianca, pianist, Hans-Jurgen Walther conducting the Pro-Musica Orchestra: M-G-M 3307 (Also: *Preludes, Second Rhapsody* and *Cuban Overture*).

The choice between the Wild-Fiedler and the Pennario-Newman versions is a difficult one. The former is performed in concert style, while the latter has a dance-band quality. Both are delightful and excellently done (and both recordings are worth having because of the fine collection of Gershwin they contain). The Weed-Whiteman is a good performance, but like the Bianca-Walther may no longer be listed in the catalogs. Unfortunately Whiteman's performance of the *Rhapsody in Blue* is marred by the use of a chorus. Likewise, the *Cuban Overture* has been tampered with, to no advantage. The M-G-M record is a more straightforward performance, but may be even more difficult to find than the Coral Record.

Catfish Row (1936)

—Maurice Abravanel conducting the Utah Symphony: Westminster 18850 (Reverse: Grofé's *Grand Canyon Suite*).

To date this is the only recording of Gershwin's own *Porgy and Bess* suite. (The *Symphonic Picture from Porgy and Bess* is an arrangement by Robert Russell Bennett.) Gershwin's *Catfish Row* is an extremely interesting work, for Gershwin not only used such familiar songs as "Summertime," "I Got Plenty o' Nothin'" and "Bess, You Is My Woman Now," but many lesser-known purely orchestral passages—the *Storm Music* and the *Fight Fugue*—and the opening piano solo that was cut from the original. The Utah Symphony performs with great spirit and the recording is excellent.

Musical Scores

Oh, Kay! (1926)

—Barbara Ruick, Jack Cassidy, Allen Case, Roger White, orchestra and chorus conducted by Lehman Engle: Columbia CL 1050.

Musical numbers: *Overture;* The Woman's Touch; Don't Ask; Dear Little Girl; Maybe; Clap Yo' Hands; Bride and Groom; Do Do Do; Someone to Watch Over Me; Fidgety Feet; Heaven on Earth; Oh, Kay; Finale.

—David Daniels, Marti Stevens, Bernie West, Eddie Phillips, others, chorus and "orchestra" conducted by Dorothea Freitag: 20th Fox 4003.

> Musical numbers: *Overture;* The Woman's Touch; The Twenties Are Here to Stay; Home; Stiff Upper Lip; Maybe; The Pophams; Do Do Do; Clap Yo' Hands; Someone to Watch Over Me; Fidgety Feet; You'll Still Be There; Little Jazz Bird; Oh, Kay; Finale.

The Columbia recording is a record revival of the original score, the 20th Fox record a recording by the off-Broadway original cast revival. Both are delights. The Columbia is faithful to the original, presenting the songs as they might have sounded in 1926, complete with a fine two-piano team. The 20th Fox album contains two songs borrowed from the score of *Primrose,* "The Twenties Are Here to Stay" (originally "When Toby Is Out of Town") and "The Pophams" (originally "The Mophams") with new lyrics by P. G. Wodehouse. Wodehouse also did new lyrics—why he did is anyone's guess—for the original *Oh, Kay!* songs, "Don't Ask" changed to "Home," and "Dear Little Girl," changed to "You'll Still Be There." "Little Jazz Bird" was borrowed from *Lady, Be Good!* (1924) and "Stiff Upper Lip" from *A Damsel in Distress* (1937). The singing in both sets is generally good and, if not good, at least in the right spirit.

Girl Crazy (1930)

> —Mary Martin, Louise Carlyle, Eddie Chappell, chorus and orchestra conducted by Lehman Engle: Columbia CL 882.
>
> Musical numbers: *Overture;* the Lonesome Cow-

boy; Bidin' My Time; Could You Use Me?; Broncho Busters; Barbary Coast; Embraceable You; Sam and Delilah; I Got Rhythm; But Not For Me; Treat Me Rough; Boy! What Love Has Done To Me!; Cactus Time in Arizona; Finale.

Even the often too-mannered singing of Mary Martin does not spoil the attractions of this album. This was one of Gershwin's best scores, a fact that was recognized even at the time. The songs are typical of the work of the Gershwins—the music is crisp; the lyrics are bright; the songs are free of sentimentality. The best singing in the album is contributed by Louise Carlyle.

Porgy and Bess (1935)

—Lawrence Winters, Camilla Williams, Inez Matthews, Warren Coleman, Avon Long, Edward Matthews, chorus and orchestra conducted by Lehman Engle: Columbia OSL-162, three long-playing records.

This is the only authentic and virtually complete recording of *Porgy and Bess* and it is an excellent one in every way, vocally, orchestrally and technically. A must for any complete Gershwin collection.

Porgy and Bess—Excerpts

—Lawrence Winters, Camilla Williams, Inez Matthews, Warren Coleman, Avon Long, Edward Matthews, chorus and orchestra conducted by Lehman Engle: Columbia CL-922.

Musical numbers: *Overture;* Summertime; A Woman Is a Sometime Thing; My Man's Gone Now; It Take a Long Pull to Get There; I Got Plenty o' Nothin'; The Buzzard Song; Bess, You Is My Woman Now; It Ain't Necessarily So; What You Want Wid Bess?; There's a Boat Dat's Leavin' Soon For New York; Oh, Where's My Bess?; I'm On My Way.

—Todd Duncan, Anne Brown, the Eva Jessye Choir, Avon Long, Edward Matthews, Helen Dowdy, William Woolfolk, orchestra under the direction of Alexander Smallens: Decca DL 9024.

Musical numbers: *Overture;* Summertime; A Woman Is a Sometime Thing; My Man's Gone Now; It Take a Long Pull to Get There; I Got Plenty o' Nothin'; The Buzzard Song; Bess, You Is My Woman Now; It Ain't Necessarily So; What You Want Wid Bess?; Strawberry Woman's Call; Crab Man's Call; I Loves You, Porgy; The Requiem; There's a Boat Dat's Leavin' Soon For New York; Porgy's Lament (Oh, Where's My Bess?) and Finale (I'm On My Way).

—Lawrence Tibbett, Helen Jepson, chorus and orchestra under the direction of Alexander Smallens: RCA Camden CAL-500.

Musical numbers: Summertime and Crap Game; A Woman Is a Sometime Thing; My Man's Gone Now; I Got Plenty o' Nothin'; The Buzzard Song; Bess, You Is My Woman Now; It Ain't Necessarily So; Oh, Where's My Bess?

—Robert McFerrin, Adele Addison, Pearl Bailey, Cab
Calloway, Brock Peters, Loulie Jean Norman,
chorus and orchestra under the direction of André
Previn: Columbia OL 5410.

Musical numbers: *Overture;* Summertime; A
Woman Is a Sometime Thing; Gone, Gone, Gone;
Oh, Little Stars; My Man's Gone Now; I Got
Plenty o' Nothin'; Bess, You Is My Woman Now;
Morning: Catfish Row; Oh, I Can't Sit Down; It
Ain't Necessarily So; I Ain't Got No Shame; What
You Want Wid Bess?; Street Cries: Strawberry
Woman and Crab Man; I Loves You, Porgy; A Red
Headed Woman; Clara, Clara; There's a Boat Dat's
Leavin' Soon For New York; Oh, Where's My
Bess?; I'm On My Way.

—Ella Fitzgerald and Louis Armstrong, orchestra conducted by Russell Garcia: Verve MG V-4011-2.

Musical numbers: *Overture;* Summertime; I
Wants to Stay Here; My Man's Gone Now; I Got
Plenty o' Nothin'; The Buzzard Song; Bess, You Is
My Woman Now; It Ain't Necessarily So; What
You Want Wid Bess?; A Woman Is a Sometime
Thing; Oh, Doctor Jesus; Street Cries: Honey
Man, Crab Man, Strawberry Woman; There's a
Boat Dat's Leavin' Soon For New York; Oh,
Where's My Bess?; I'm On My Way.

—Miles Davis, trumpet, with orchestra under the direction of Gil Evans: Columbia CL 1274.

Musical numbers: The Buzzard Song; Bess, You
Is My Woman Now; Gone, Gone, Gone; Summertime; Oh, Where's My Bess?; Oh, Doctor Jesus;

Street Cries: Strawberry Woman, Crab Man; My
Man's Gone Now; Honey Man's Cry; I Loves You,
Porgy; There's a Boat Dat's Leavin' Soon For New
York.

Of these *Porgy and Bess* excerpt albums, the first
(Columbia CL-922) was taken from the complete album above. The Decca album was recorded in the
1940s by members of the successful revival, many of
whom appeared in the original 1935 production. Todd
Duncan and Anne Brown were the original Porgy and
Bess, chosen by Gershwin to sing the roles. The recording therefore is quite historic. So is the Camden
album starring Lawrence Tibbett; it was supervised by
Gershwin himself a few days after *Porgy and Bess*
opened in New York. The next album is from the
sound track of the movie version of *Porgy and Bess;* it
is gloriously sung, but is highly Hollywoodized in the
orchestrations which, unfortunately, are not Gershwin's
as in the other above albums. The Ella Fitzgerald—Louis
Armstrong album is interesting if only because it is
sung by these two fine jazz stylists. The interpretations
(arranged by conductor Garcia) are not authentic, but
they are always excellent listening, often beautiful and
occasionally moving. The same may be said for the
modern jazz interpretation by trumpeter Miles Davis,
who demonstrates what can be done in a true jazz sense
by taking the original Gershwin songs as a point of
departure. He is given brilliant orchestral backing and
arrangements by the talented Gil Evans.

Song Collections

The George and Ira Gershwin Song Books

—Ella Fitzgerald, orchestra conducted by Nelson Riddle: Verve MG V-4029-5.

Musical numbers: Sam and Delilah; But Not For Me; My One and Only; Let's Call the Whole Thing Off; Beginner's Luck; Oh, Lady Be Good!; Nice Work If You Can Get It; Things Are Looking Up; Just Another Rhumba; How Long Has This Been Going On?; 'S Wonderful; The Man I Love; That Certain Feeling; By Strauss; Someone to Watch Over Me; The Real American Folk Song; Who Cares?; Looking For a Boy; They All Laughed; My Cousin in Milwaukee; Somebody From Somewhere; A Foggy Day; Clap Yo' Hands; For You, For Me, For Evermore; Stiff Upper Lip; Boy Wanted; Strike Up the Band; Soon; I've Got a Crush On You; Bidin' My Time; Aren't You Kind of Glad We Did?; Of Thee I sing; The Half of It, Dearie Blues; I was Doing All Right; He Loves and She Loves; Love Is Sweeping the Country; Treat Me Rough; Love Is Here to Stay; Slap That Bass; Isn't It a Pity?; Shall We Dance?; Love Walked In; You've Got What Gets Me; They Can't Take That Away From Me; Embraceable You; I Can't Be Bothered Now; Boy! What Love Has Done to Me!; Fascinating Rhythm; Funny Face; The Lorelei; Oh So Nice; Let's Kiss and Make Up; I Got Rhythm.

The impressive singing of Ella Fitzgerald and the arrangements of Nelson Riddle make this an outstanding collection of Gershwin songs. There are more than fifty songs in this five-record set (the records are also available singly), which also brings with it a bonus record containing among other things the famous "Walking the Dog" music from *Shall We Dance?*, here titled *Promenade*. Of special importance is the inclusion of such lesser-known Gershwin songs as "The Real American Folk Song," "Boy Wanted," "You've Got What Gets Me," "Just Another Rhumba" and others. There is also a superb book on the Gershwins written by Lawrence D. Stewart.

George Gershwin at the Piano

—George Gershwin, pianist: 20th Fox 3013 (Reverse: *Rhapsody in Blue*).

Musical numbers: That Certain Feeling (Gershwin); Left All Alone Again Blues (Kern); Grieving For You (Coslow); I'm a Lonesome Little Raindrop (Hanley); Just Snap Your Fingers at Care (Silvers); *Strike Up the Band* Rehearsal—Hangin' Around With You, Strike Up the Band; Mademoiselle in New Rochelle (Gershwin); I Got Rhythm (Gershwin).

This remarkable collection assembles several Gershwin piano rolls made while the composer was still an unknown pianist. These are the only recordings made of Gershwin playing the works of other composers, including a wonderful Kern song, "Left All Alone Again Blues." The *Strike Up the Band* rehearsal, in which Gershwin exchanges quips with comedian Bobby

Clark, was transcribed from a newsreel, as was the performance of "I Got Rhythm." The early piano rolls betray their source but the later "That Certain Feeling" sounds like an actual performance, as does the *Rhapsody in Blue* on the reverse side of the record.

The Gershwin Years

—Paula Stewart, Richard Hayes, Lynn Roberts, orchestra and chorus under the direction of George Bassman: Decca DX Z-160.

Musical numbers: When You Want 'Em You Can't Get 'Em, When You've Got 'Em You Don't Want 'Em; *Rialto Ripples;* Some Wonderful Sort of Someone; I Was So Young; Nobody But You; Swanee; Do It Again; I'll Build a Stairway to Paradise; I Won't Say I Will; Oh, Lady Be Good!; Fascinating Rhythm; So Am I; The Man I Love; Sweet and Low-Down; Looking For a Boy; That Certain Feeling; Maybe; Clap Yo' Hands; Do Do Do; Someone to Watch Over Me; High Hat; He Loves and She Loves; 'S Wonderful; My One and Only; How Long Has This Been Going On?; Oh So Nice; I Don't Think I'll Fall in Love Today; Where's the Boy?; Feeling I'm Falling; Do What You Do!; Liza; I've Got a Crush on You; Soon; Strike Up the Band; Embraceable You; Could You Use Me?; But Not For Me; Bidin' My Time; I Got Rhythm; Of Thee I Sing; Who Cares?; Love Is Sweeping the Country; The Lorelei; Isn't It a Pity?; My Cousin in Milwaukee; Mine; Summertime; There's a Boat Dat's Leavin' Soon For New York; Bess, You Is My

Woman Now; Let's Call the Whole Thing Off; They Can't Take That Away From Me; They All Laughed; A Foggy Day; Nice Work If You Can Get It; Love Walked In; Love Is Here to Stay.

This excellent set (three records) covers Gershwin's output from his first published song to the last. Handsomely produced and well sung, it is the only collection that attempts a chronological survey of Gershwin's song writing. Bassman's arrangements and conducting reveal a deep insight into the works of Gershwin. Happily, there are no stars in this album, except Gershwin.

SELECTED BIBLIOGRAPHY

Armitage, Merle, *George Gershwin*. Longmans, Green & Co., 1938.

Ewen, David, *A Journey to Greatness: The Life and Music of George Gershwin*. Henry Holt & Co., 1956.

Gershwin, Ira, *Lyrics on Several Occasions*. Alfred A. Knopf, 1959.

Goldberg, Isaac, *George Gershwin: A Study in American Music*. Simon and Schuster, Inc., 1931; reissued, with a supplement by Edith Garson, by the Frederick Ungar Publishing Co., 1958.

Jablonski, Edward, and Stewart, Lawrence D., *The Gershwin Years*. Doubleday & Co., 1958.

Music collected in book form

Gershwin, George, *George Gershwin's Song Book*. Simon and Schuster, Inc., 1932.

Gershwin, George, and Ira, *The George and Ira Gershwin Song Book*. Simon and Schuster, Inc., 1960.

Published vocal scores of shows

Primrose, lyrics by Desmond Carter and Ira Gershwin. Chappell & Co., Ltd. (London), 1924.

Strike Up the Band, lyrics by Ira Gershwin. New World Music Corp., 1930.

Girl Crazy, lyrics by Ira Gershwin. New World Music Corp., 1954.

Of Thee I Sing, lyrics by Ira Gershwin. New World Music Corp., 1932.

Porgy and Bess, lyrics by DuBose Heyward and Ira Gershwin. Gershwin Publishing Corp., 1935.

GLOSSARY OF MUSICAL AND
THEATRICAL TERMS

ARIA	A song, especially if sung in an opera.
BALLAD	Tin Pan Alley term for popular love song.
BLUE NOTE	Those notes in jazz music that sound deliberately flat (off key), but which give the blues its characteristic sound. In a blues scale the third and seventh degrees are the blue notes.
BLUES	The "sorrow songs" of the Negroes, usually in slow tempo and using blue notes.
BOOK SHOW	A musical comedy for which a plot exists; not a revue which consists of a series of unrelated numbers.
CADENZA	The passages for the soloist in a concerto (piano, violin, etc.) in which the player is permitted to show off his technique.
CHORD	The sounding together of any two or more related notes simultaneously, thus producing harmony.

CHORUS In popular music the important part of the song. The verse is the introductory part but is rarely sung.

COUNTERPOINT The art of writing music which combines several parts to be performed at the same time. Contrapuntal music may have different parts of the orchestra playing different melodies at the same time.

DEVICE Any of the many purely technical musical means of achieving a musical effect.

DISSONANCE The clashing of two notes that do not go together, that do not harmonize.

FINALE The closing section of a musical work.

HARMONY The art of combining the different sounds of music in a composition.

MELODY A combination of notes, one following the other, that makes musical sense. The tune of a song.

MOTIF A short musical idea, usually not a complete melody.

OPENERS The opening numbers of musical comedy acts. Very lively and attention-catching; also called "icebreakers."

ORCHESTRATION The art of using instruments in a musical work, singly and in combination. Involves deciding on what instrument or instruments should play certain passages, etc.

PIANO COPY The composer's version of a song written out for voice with piano accompaniment.

RECITATIVE That portion of the opera which is neither actually sung nor spoken, but is chanted over an instrumental accompaniment.

REVUE A form of musical comedy without a plot; consists of skits and musical numbers.

RHYTHM — The heartbeat of music, the musical motion that carries the music along. Not to be confused with tempo, which determines the speed of a musical work.

RHYTHM NUMBER — A musical number that does not depend upon melody for its effect. Usually sung at a fast tempo, thus the rhythm is more pronounced.

SYNCOPATION — A rhythmic trick of shifting the emphasis from the customary note (usually the first of the bar) to another weaker note. This upsets the usual equal grouping of beats in a composition.

THEME — An important musical idea (a melody or motif) of a composition. The theme is what the musical work is about.

TONE POEM — A composition that tries to tell a story in music. Not considered as important as "abstract music," which does not attempt storytelling.

TRANSPOSE — To change the key of a musical work, or song. If the latter, it requires musical skill to transpose the song from its written key into another key.

TRYOUT — The testing of a show out of town before bringing it into New York for its official premiere.

VERSE — The introductory section of a popular song; rarely sung. We generally only hear the chorus, plus its middle called the "release."

INDEX

185